NOLA BARRON

potter, sculptor, gallery director

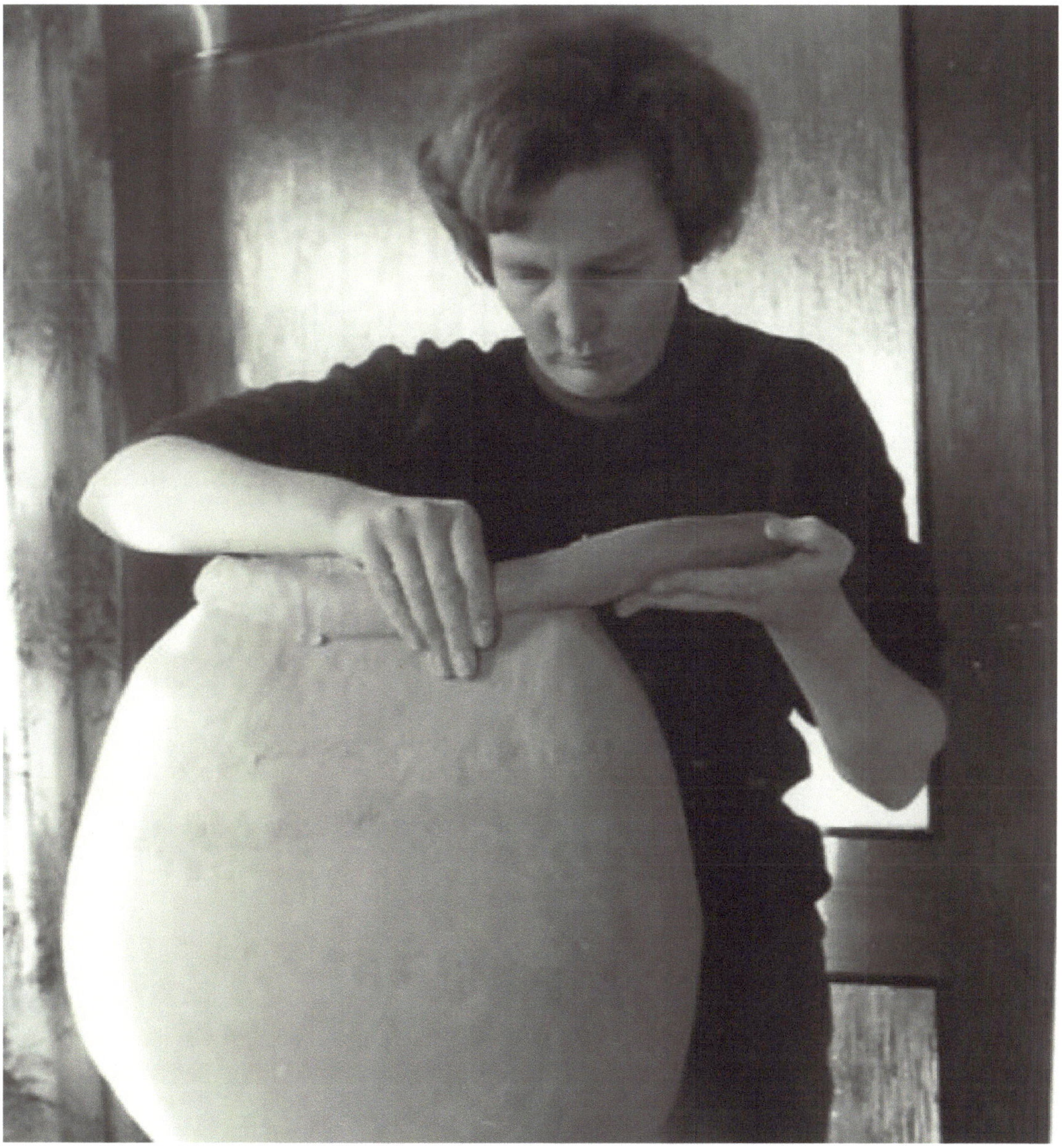

Written by Nola and Owen Barron. Introduction by Grant Banbury

Copyright © March 2020

Edition 1.0

This book is copyright. Except for the purposes of fair review, no part may be stored or transmitted in any form or by any means, electronic or mechanical, including recording or storage in any information retrieval system, without permission in writing from the author or publishers. No reproduction may be made, whether by photocopying or by any other means, unless a licence has been obtained from the author, publisher or their agent.

ISBN 978-0-473-51729-8

Cover design: John Burt

Cover image: People pot, stoneware, h 332 mm. The last of the series. Photo: Nola Barron Archives

Nola Barron wrote

'Clova, the country kitten who came to the city,' 2018. A story for children about coping with the loss of a pet or a loved one. ISBN 1986188191.

Owen Barron wrote

'Night Watchman and other stories from New Zealand.' A small collection of short stories and poems. ISBN 9781533091147.

'Pharmacy Practice and Practicing Pharmacists.' A history pf pharmacy and local pharmacists in Christchurch from 1850 to 2000. ISBN 9780473189945.

'Ships and Sealing Wax, Recollections of Owen Barron.' A biography. No ISBN.

CONTENTS

ABOUT THIS BOOK

This book is a record of the artistic career of Nola Barron. It covers three different aspects of her life and works. After an initial interest in painting, she found that pottery was the craft she wished to follow. She enrolled at the Studio of Design, which was established by Yvonne Rust, an influential New Zealand potter, and learned the basics of throwing, glazing and firing stoneware pottery. After about two years of tuition, she established her own studio and built a kiln. Not satisfied with wheel-thrown domestic objects she experimented with hand-built forms of a more decorative nature, using clay to produce sculptural shapes. She also made ceramic tiles which were assembled and mounted on plywood to make decorative panels.

Wishing to expand her knowledge, Nola enrolled as a part-time student at the University of Canterbury School of Fine Arts where she studied design and sculpture. She also extended her range of materials, producing sculptures in fibreglass, cast aluminium and cast bronze. Some of these objects were produced from clay moulds.

During her career as a potter and sculptor, Nola Barron achieved success and acceptance of both her peers and the public. Her work also received the approbation of critics. She exhibited widely throughout New Zealand over a long period and sold work through a number of outlets. Her work is included in several public collections and she received commissions from both private clients and commercial collectors. She was recognised as an honorary member of both the Canterbury Potters Association and the New Zealand Society of Potters.

In 1977 Nola Barron was appointed director of the Canterbury Society of Arts (CSA) Gallery. This was an entirely different challenge and responsibility, which she found most rewarding. During her 10-year term (1977-1986) the gallery held an average of 90 exhibitions a year, attracting large gatherings of supporters. Around 25 per cent of these shows featured fine crafts in group or solo exhibitions. The gallery was also a leader in the promotion of non-object or performance art.

ABOUT THE AUTHOR

Nola Alison Campbell was born in Christchurch, New Zealand on July 7, 1931. She attended several Christchurch primary schools and Christchurch Girls' High School. On leaving high school, she served a four-year apprenticeship in a Christchurch pharmacy. Nola and her future husband, Owen Barron, met as fellow students in 1949. In 1951, Nola Campbell was secretary of the Canterbury Pharmacy Students Association and Owen was president. They married in 1952 and established their community practice, Barron's Pharmacy Ltd, in Shirley, Christchurch in 1953. They have three sons (two surviving) and three grandchildren.

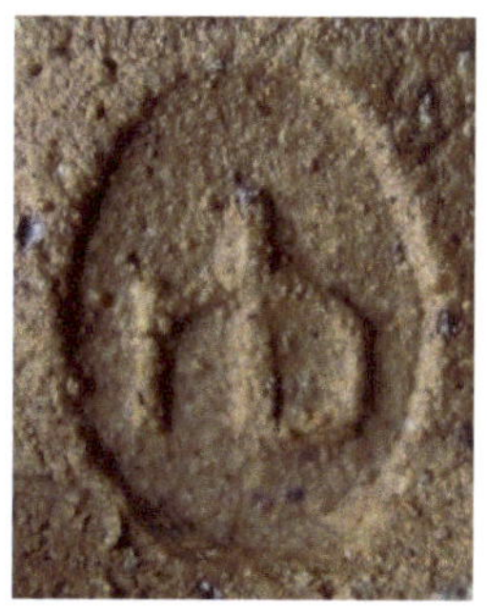

Nola Barron's potter's mark

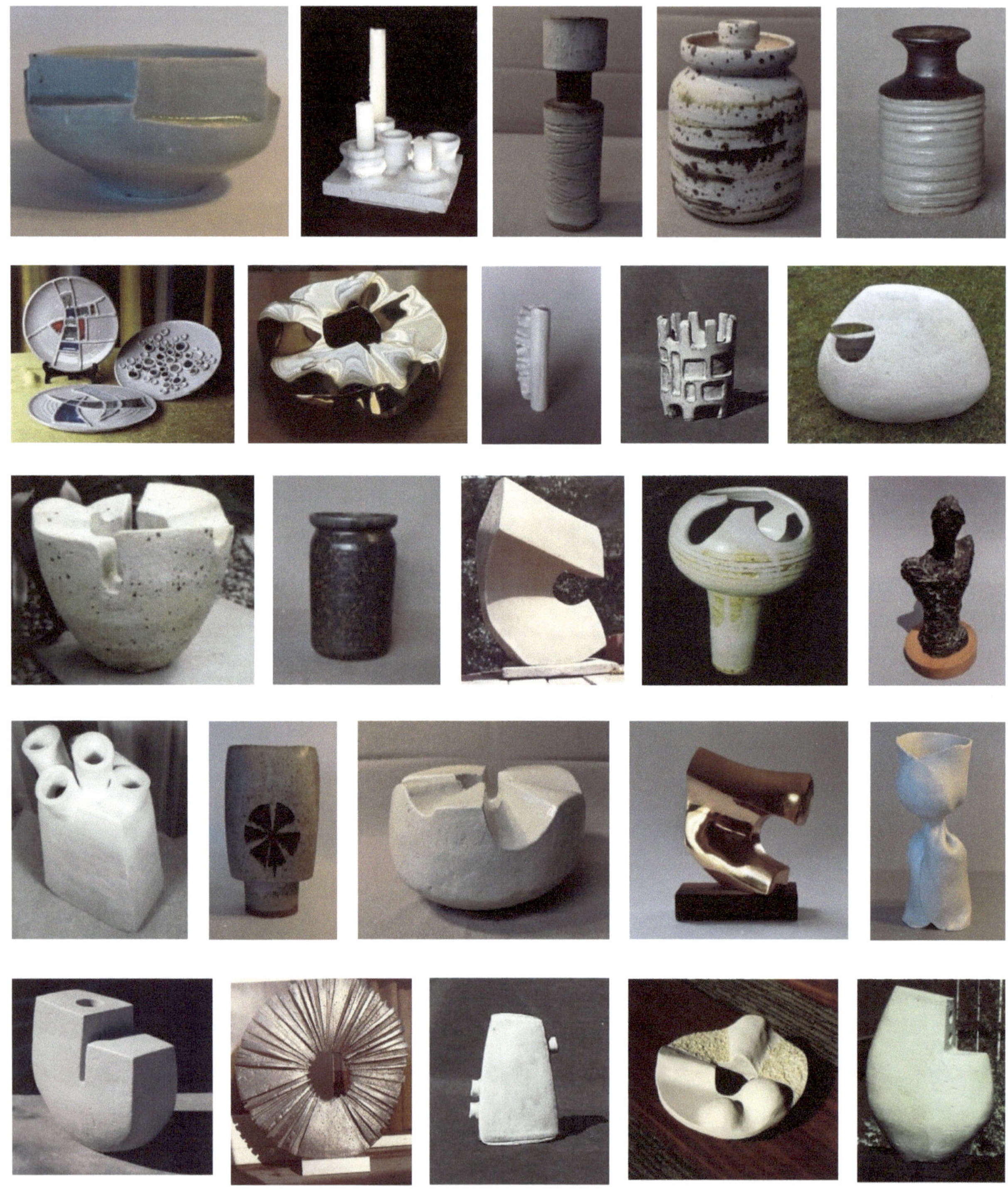

Copies of this book are available by email from nobarron@xtra.co.nz , zl3dw@outlook.co.nz , or from Amazon https://www.amazon.com/Barron-potter-sculptor-gallery-director/dp/0473517299/

INTRODUCTION BY GRANT BANBURY

'The sculptor must search with passionate intensity for the underlying principle of the organisation of mass and tension – the meaning of gesture and structure of rhythm.'
Barbara Hepworth.

Nola Barron was involved from the beginning of the pottery movement in Canterbury in the 1950s and a founding member of Canterbury Potters Association in 1963 – part of the initial wave of development recognised today as New Zealand studio pottery. She went on to exhibit her ceramics for three decades in local and New Zealand Society of Potters' national exhibitions, invitational shows and on occasions was a selector.

By the late 1960s she was invited to become a member of The Group in Christchurch, and from 1977 to 1986 played a pivotal role as director of the CSA Gallery. Determined to include exhibitions of craft, ceramics and applied arts, she facilitated a thriving programme.

During that time, I worked with her at the gallery in my capacity as exhibition officer. In terms of pottery, a large and hugely successful show by UK potter Alan Caiger-Smith in 1977 remains a highlight under her directorship. And in 1985, I purchased my first Len Castle pot from a stunning solo exhibition Nola organised.

Nola's pottery output was not large. She produced domestic-scale functional pots – bowls, lidded-jars, winged vases, elegantly proportioned candlesticks and exquisite sculptural pieces in porcelain – some small enough to fit into your hand. And, like many potters at this time, she sold work readily through retail craft outlets in Christchurch and Canterbury. Gaining confidence, she increased the scale of her work, producing stand-alone sculptural forms and, later, a series of low-relief bronzes based on landscape profiles, often repeating rhythmical forms. With highly polished surfaces these pieces sparkle and gleam, as if denying the weight of the metal.

Her large hand-built stoneware forms, often experimental, are distinctive sculptures. In contract to smaller works, they appear abstract. In some, Nola employed precise cuts, indentations and holes, puncturing otherwise plain surfaces to create surprising tensions within each piece.

Modernist in approach and outlook, Nola's sculptural works sit apart from much that was produced during the heyday of New Zealand studio ceramics, mostly dominated by functional domestic ware. Now, decades later, her work merits fresh analysis; fresh dialogue in positioning her contribution in the broad context of 20th-century New Zealand ceramics. What is it that makes Nola's pots sing? What do the forms suggest and what conceptual threads underpin her output? Experienced today, Nola's best work resonates with a rare integrity.

By the late 1960s, her work was beginning to be recognised. In 1967, noted painter Don Peebles observed: 'What has appealed about this potter's work … is its ability to stand as form worth experiencing for its own sake'.[1]

Over time Nola's use of a simple white glaze became her signature, cleverly directing the viewer's attention to form rather than decoration. Her circular Ring Landform (1972), one of a series, is powerful.

---

[1] D.P. [Peebles], "Potters' Exhibition", **The Press**, July 31, 1967, p. 14.

An energised statement about our land, where the undulating forms create rhythmical movement, counterbalanced by containment, open yet enclosed and her People Pots are distinctive and individual.

Barron's take feels modernist. Her output suggests knowledge of international art movements yet during interviews Nola's reluctance to discuss influences or acknowledge any direct reference to other potters' intrigues. A constructive parallel can be drawn between Nola's sculptural forms and that of English-born sculptor Barbara Hepworth's practice and, in 1985, it must have been a revelation for Nola to step inside Hepworth's St Ives home/studio in Cornwall.

At the time of writing, only ten ceramic works by Nola Barron are held in public collections: Christchurch Art Gallery Te Puna o Waiwhetū has four, Canterbury Museum two, Whanganui's Quartz Museum of Studio Ceramics, set up by noted potter Rick Rudd, has four, and the University of Canterbury has a bronze sculpture.

Grant Banbury, March 2020.

ACKNOWLEDGEMENTS

I wish to acknowledge particular friends in the arts who supplied moral encouragement and support, and who generously shared with me much hard-earned information and experience.

These included Ria Bancroft, Doris Lusk, Don Peebles, Pat Mulcahy, David Brokenshire, and Rosemary Perry. Having people appreciate your work enough to buy it is satisfying, although I have found that while praise from uninformed quarters, however enthusiastically presented, is pleasant to receive it does not rank with that from a small group whose opinions you respect.

I am grateful to those who helped with the production of this book. I also wish to express my appreciation of the following people who donated valuable time in helping with the production of this book. Without their generous assistance, it would not have been possible.

Grant Banbury, who researched archives of Ceramics New Zealand, Canterbury Society of Arts, Canterbury Potters Association, Christchurch Art Gallery Te Puna o Waiwhetū, private collections, and other sources for details of exhibitions and reviews. Also, for his assistance with editing the book and for his insightful introduction to my work. Rosa Shiels who edited the manuscript and made several useful suggestions. John Burt who designed the cover, and John Collie for photography. Andrew and Carol Barron who formatted the manuscript and submitted it for publishing. But mainly, my husband Owen for his love, continuing support and encouragement in all things.

SECTION ONE **POTTER**

When I left Christchurch Girls' High School in 1948 my ambition was to follow a career involving designing and making things. Possibly because my father was a builder, my thoughts turned to architecture. At that time the study in architecture was available only at the University of Auckland. When it was decided that my attendance there was impractical, I enrolled in a four-year pharmacy apprenticeship. The first opportunity I had to develop my interest in art was in 1953 and 1954 when I attended painting classes with John Oakley held at the WEA (Workers Education Association) in Christchurch. I cannot recall when my involvement with pottery began. I do remember being impressed by a Mirek Smíšek bowl for sale at the General Trading Company in Cashel Street. Perhaps it was that bowl which sparked my interest.

Pottery in New Zealand

Most civilizations have a tradition of making objects from fired clay dating back thousands of years. For example, there are references to potters and pottery in ancient manuscripts, including the Bible.[2]

The original inhabitants of this country, the Māori, who originated in Polynesia, were skilled at using wood and shells to make vessels and at carving stone for ornaments and weapons, but there is no record of them using clay. Pottery in New Zealand is no older than the first European settlement in the early 19th century.

When brickworks became established, some workers experimented with making domestic pottery ware in conjunction with their main business of manufacturing pipes and bricks. Some amateur potters produced earthenware pots in the 1920s, but few examples of this work have been preserved.[3] In the mid-1940s, after the Second World War, there were several professional potters in New Zealand making a living from producing and selling pottery. The increased demand for hand-made domestic ware was partly due to a scarcity of good quality imported pottery. Also, interest was generated by New Zealanders who had seen and bought examples of pottery while travelling overseas.

Early New Zealand potters

This list is not a complete record of all those working with clay at that time. No doubt there are some potters whose names should be included. I apologise for any omissions. I was fortunate to become familiar with the work of the following pottery pioneers. In Auckland, a group of potters, including Len Castle, Barry Brickell, Margaret Milne and Patricia Perrin, were actively engaged in making pottery and teaching beginners. In Wellington, people interested in pottery were inspired by Roy and Juliet Cowan (Peter), Terrence Barrow, Elizabeth Matheson, Doreen Blumhardt, and Muriel Moody. Nelson had English potter Jack Laird and Mirek Smíšek, a Czechoslovakian who had immigrated via Australia and set up a pottery. Laird introduced pottery to a wide audience through his demonstrations on Television New Zealand.

In 1962, Harry and May Davis arrived to build their Crewena pottery at Wakapuaka near Nelson. The Davises were established potters from England, where their 'Crowan Pottery' produced domestic ware of consistently high quality. They had also started a pottery in South America where they hoped

---

[2] Jeremaiah 18: *'Go down to the potter's house and there I will give you my message.'*
[3] Noeline Brokenshire, **Fired Clay: The story of the Canterbury Potters Association 1870-1999**, Christchurch, 1999.

to inspire the local people to re-establish an industry which had once flourished in their community. Harry and May brought a different philosophy to the production of useful vessels. They believed pottery should be inexpensive and affordable to most of the population. The quality of the domestic ware they made set a standard to which many new potters aspired. They showed it was possible to make a living from the craft.

Pottery in Canterbury

Several people were influential in fostering pottery in Christchurch. These included Wyn Reed, Doris Holland (Lusk), and Margaret Frankel. But one person who stood out as an inspiration was Yvonne Rust.[4] Yvonne had graduated with a Diploma of Fine Arts and was employed by the Adult Education Department. In 1956, having been captivated by a demonstration of pottery making by Robert N. Field in Dunedin, Yvonne organised a national pottery school in Christchurch.

She invited most of the people involved with clay in New Zealand at that time, borrowed 50 pottery wheels and engaged Patricia Perrin, Carl Vendelbosch, Marian Mauger, Mirek Smíšek and Jim Nelson as tutors. More than 80 people attended the school. For many, it was their first introduction to pottery and a number went on to make a career in the field.

I decided to investigate this craft. Yvonne Rust and Jim Nelson were providing pottery classes at a 'craft centre' at 116 Springfield Road, Christchurch, but there were no vacancies. Subsequently, that partnership was dissolved, and Yvonne moved to a studio in Cashel Street where I enrolled as a painting student. Then in 1962, Yvonne moved from Cashel Street and established her Studio of Design in a large, ramshackle building at 1038 North Colombo Street. The building had been a furniture factory and was in poor condition. It was draughty, with a rough concrete floor and a leaky roof.

It was here that I first tried my hand at pottery. There was no formal tuition. In fact, my first teacher was a young student, Colin Strange, who was only a few steps ahead of the class. Utter chaos prevailed, but what Yvonne lacked in technical knowledge was compensated for by her boundless enthusiasm, devotion and determination. It was very much a case of sharing knowledge and trial and error. Nobody knew much, so we all muddled along, learning and exchanging information as we went. This is probably the reason my work was never particularly conventional.

Yvonne was determined to build a kiln capable of reaching the stoneware temperature of 1300 degrees centigrade. After several unsuccessful attempts, this was achieved. A drip-fed, oil-fired kiln was built but, as it belched black smoke and soot over the neighbourhood, it could be fired only at night. In spite of the rather primitive equipment, a lot of fine and worthwhile pottery was produced.

Under the influence of Bernard Leach and Yvonne Rust, we made stoneware pottery glazed with ash and rock glazes and fired at high temperature. The glazes were mainly brown, black or grey, which relied on small miracles in the firing process to become special. The atmosphere within the kiln, either oxidising or reducing, often produced different results from the same glaze.

There was no facility for the formal study of pottery making in New Zealand until a three-year, full-time course was established at Otago Polytechnic in the 1980s. Prior to this, an aspiring potter had two avenues for learning the craft. One was to obtain an apprenticeship by working alongside an established potter in his or her workshop, but as there few professional potters practising at that time this was unusual. Most students learned by attending classes with tutors often sponsored by

---

[4] Theresa Sjoquist, **Yvonne Rust: Maverick Spirit,** David Ling, 2011.

community centres or privately established art schools. The level of tuition varied according to the skill of the tutor. The main benefit was the provision of facilities – pottery wheels, clay and other materials, and a kiln for firing finished pots. Students learned by trial and error and helping each other.

The situation has been described well by author Peter Cape

'It was and perhaps still is one of the notable aspects of pottery in New Zealand that formal tuition has always taken second place and the main emphasis has been on experience and the interchange of ideas. It was this latter which characterised the development in the early forties and fifties. There was a strong family feeling among those who worked clay with their hands. … To anybody who has followed the course of craft pottery in New Zealand and who is able to look back over thirty years of development, it is the fellowship, the exchange of technical ideas and know-how; the kiln-building parties and the communal firings during the first twenty years, which stand out as much as the improving quality of the pots produced.'[5]

This 'family feeling' was still evident in the 1960s when I started making pottery and I appreciated being part of it.

Canterbury Potters Association

A Christchurch couple, Alan and Wyn Reed had bought pottery overseas and donated some works to Canterbury Museum. They became interested in establishing the craft in Christchurch. Due to the Reeds' foresight, the Canterbury Potters Association (CPA) was formed in April 1963. The inaugural meeting was held at Risingholme Community Centre with 37 foundation members, who were practising potters or people interested in this comparatively new to New Zealand craft form. I was a foundation member of the association and served on the committee as treasurer for a number of years.

Several years later, I was honoured to be offered life membership of the association. Members of CPA were active in promoting the new craft. We arranged for a number of highly regarded overseas potters to lecture and demonstrate their skills. We were all thirsty for knowledge and there is no doubt that these visits were of benefit to all who attended.

Lectures and demonstrations

As there was little information available for budding potters, we took every opportunity to expand our knowledge. Initially, lectures were delivered by international experts but, as New Zealand potters became proficient and achieved international recognition, they were invited to be guest potters and selectors for the annual exhibitions. They were also asked to give workshops and talk about particular aspects of the craft to local potters.

I attended almost all of these schools and lectures (mostly illustrated). I appreciated the work of these potters and was interested in their points of view, but I had no wish to make conventional pots or copy any particular style or shape. Although none of them affected my designs directly; it was often the intangible things that were of value. My concern was to extend the possibilities of working with clay by designing and making unique forms which were radically different from those being made by other practitioners.

---

[5] Peter Cape, Please Touch: A survey of the three-dimensional arts New Zealand, William Collins, 1980, p. 80.

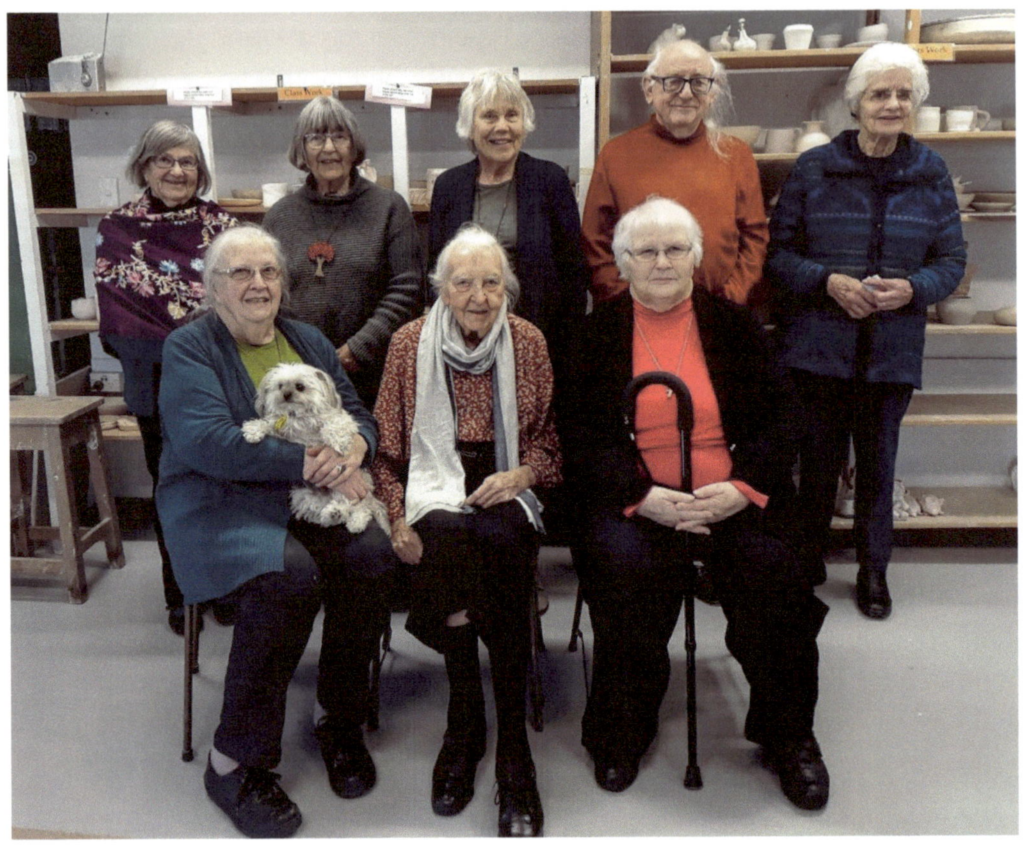

Canterbury Potters Association Life Members
CPA Rooms, Christchurch, September 15, 2019
From left, standing: Rosemary Thompson, Margaret Ryley, Sally Connolly, Jim Pollard,
Rosemary Perry
Seated: Frederika Ernsten, Nola Barron, Maureen Johnston
Photo: Ngarita Wight & Trish Morant

In 1964 the CPA arranged visits by international experts Takeichi Kawai from Japan and John Kingston from the US. Both were leading potters in their respective countries, but with different attitudes to the craft. John Kingston, a sculptor, presented a workshop. I was impressed with his freedom to use new ideas and techniques, and the depth of his vision. It allowed me to see the bigger picture. He worked in wood with a chainsaw, as well as in clay.

Annual exhibitions

From its inception, the CPA established an annual pottery exhibition held either in the CSA Gallery or Canterbury Museum. These presentations continue today at Canterbury Museum. Work is submitted to a selection committee or an individual selector, to ensure that the exhibited works meet a high standard. These exhibitions attract numbers of interested people and many of the works on view are sold. In addition to being an exhibitor, I was often involved in setting up these shows, usually as a member of the selection panel.

Shōji Hamada (1894-1978)

Perhaps our most prestigious visitor was Shōji Hamada, who came to Christchurch with his son, Atsuya, in 1965 to present a workshop and talk about his work.

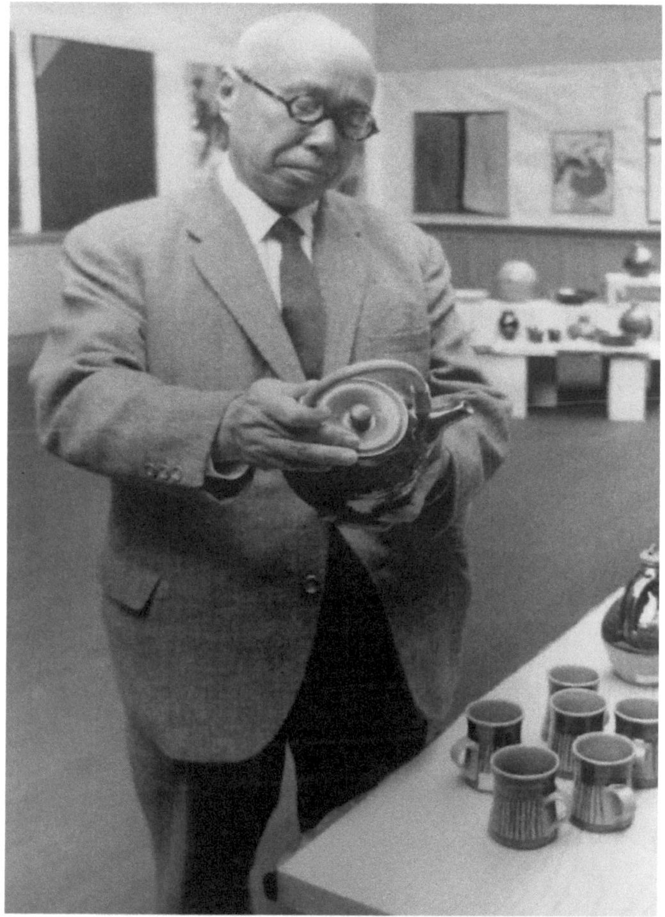

Shōji Hamada appraising a teapot

Revered as a National Treasure by the Japanese, Shōji Hamada is regarded as one of the leading potters of the world. He brought with him examples of his work produced in Japan and, while he was in New Zealand, made and fired pots at Yvonne Rust's studio. Some of the Japanese-made pots were sold by ballot and some were donated to the Canterbury and Auckland museums. The pots made in New Zealand were donated to local potters who had assisted him. It was an opportunity to own works that would have been highly valued in Japan. The objects made here were considered to be especially important, as they were actually made by the master. Much of his work in Japan was made by others and decorated by Hamada. I had the honour of driving Shōji Hamada from his accommodation to and from the studio where he was working. I found him to be both humble and inspiring. I was conscious of having such an important person in my care and worried that any transgression on my part could have initiated an international incident. One concept he explained to me was the comparative roles of an artist and a critic. He likened the situation to climbing two sides of a pyramid. Both the artist and the critic should be at the same level of accomplishment and understanding.

Bernard Leach (1887-1979)

The practice of studio pottery in New Zealand, which had begun after World War II, received a welcome boost when Bernard Leach toured the country in 1962. Leach was an English potter of considerable repute. He established a pottery in St Ives, Cornwall in 1920. Leach's book, 'A Potter's Book,' was the first book about modern pottery and was regarded as the potters' bible. In addition to describing the art of making pottery, the book contained detailed practical information, such as how to make potters' wheels and instructions for building and firing a pottery kiln. Bernard Leach made eight trips to Japan and lived there for over four years. He worked alongside several of the leading Japanese potters, including Shōji Hamada. It was at this time that he experienced the 'philosophy' of pottery as understood in that country. Leach's book and lectures inspired many New Zealand potters to take up the craft and join the small number of established full-time professional potters working at that time. However, few of us were at the stage where we could appreciate or profit from his higher ideals and plane of discernment.

New Zealand Society of Potters (NZSP)

The NZSP was formed in October 1963. It became an Incorporated Society in 1965 (**New Zealand Potter**s Inc.) and is now Ceramics New Zealand. The first national exhibition of pottery, organised by Oswald C. Stephens, was held in Dunedin's Otago Museum in 1957. Annual exhibitions followed in Wellington (1958), Christchurch (1959), and Auckland (1960), and continue to the present time. Initially, to qualify for membership of this society, potters were required to attain certain standards. Pots were submitted for the annual exhibitions and assessed by a selection panel. If considered acceptable, they were included in the exhibition. Initially only exhibiting potters were eligible for membership. This requirement is no longer in place.

In 1964 I submitted pots to the NZSP for inclusion in its eighth annual exhibition. Four pots were accepted and my membership to the society was confirmed. Later I became Canterbury's delegate to the committee of the NZSP and, as such, attended annual meetings, which were held in conjunction with the Annual Exhibition in various centres throughout the country. I was awarded honorary membership of the NZSP in 1997.

Magazines

Helen Mason was the first editor of **New Zealand Potter** magazine, first published in 1958. Six years later she wrote an article in **Salient**, the Victoria University student paper, entitled "Pottery in New Zealand." Published twice yearly until 1998, **New Zealand Potter** continued under different names including **Clay News.** It is now **Ceramics New Zealand**. Such magazines are valuable tools for exchanging information, exhibitions reviews including Ceramics New Zealand's annual exhibitions, and publishing articles and photographs of work by leading potters. Eventually, more written information became available from overseas publishers, such as Thames & Hudson. All articles were appreciated by enthusiastic potters who were conscious of gaining as much knowledge as possible.

A studio of my own

My serious involvement with pottery dates from the establishment of a workshop at home in Shirley. We added a small room to our garage and fitted it out with a sink, benches and shelves. All the necessary tools were made or purchased. I bought a pottery wheel from Leon Cohen, of Seaboard Joinery in Christchurch, who was making wheels to a Bernard Leach design.

Following a plan by Roy Cowan, and refined by David Brokenshire, we built a fire-brick, two-chambered, oil-fired kiln at the back of the section. It was fired with a 'pot-burner' to pre-heat, then switched to an air-forced Venturi burner to take the temperature up to 1300°C. It was a marvellous little kiln right from the start. The second chamber produced biscuit-fired pots ready for glazing at the same time that glazed pots were fired in the first chamber, so there was a cycle of production. It took approximately 10 hours to reach maximum heat, with constant monitoring using a pyrometer and by observing test cones in the kiln which melt at specific temperatures. I obtained clay from Nelson. Mirek Smíšek was making his own clay and taught Ian McPherson, the owner of clay deposits at Mapua, how to blend and prepare it. Ian supplied ready-to-use clay and clay in powder form to potters who reconstituted it for use. For my early domestic work, I used glazes recommended by Bernard Leach. These were made from a combination of wood ash, acting as a flux, combined with minerals (ground-up rock) and various oxides to impart colour.

Every kiln-load I fired included test clays or glazes, as I was interested in extending the medium in new ways. Whenever we travelled in New Zealand, I brought back rocks, such as serpentine from the Nelson area, to be ground up for test glazes. Most rocks produce various shades of brown due to the iron content, but one stone from Franz Josef Glacier resulted in a nice mottled, dark-green effect rather like the West Coast bush. Later, I coated my larger sculptural pieces with a matt-white glaze based on a formula called "Rhodes 32" from a book by Daniel Rhodes[6], as I found that it enhanced the sculptural aspect of my work. This glaze contained feldspar, China clay (kaolin) dolomite and whiting.

Function versus form

Along with most of my contemporaries, I started out making domestic stoneware – bowls, candlesticks, vases, storage jars, and plates – thrown on the Leach kick-wheel. I soon became interested in producing hand-built forms, which allowed more individuality. My main criteria were that the results should be satisfying to the eye.

The statement, "great minds think unalike", amused me and possibly inspired me to be different. My work became more sculptural and experimental with an emphasis on form rather than function. With the intention of extending the limitations of clay as a medium, I worked on a series of designs originating in my imagination. I visualised a shape then attempted to reproduce it in clay, expanding each design idea into a series of works based around a common theme. The original concept was modified until I was satisfied that it could not be extended any further. Then I worked on a new idea. Sometimes my imagination was triggered by current events. For instance, after the first successful heart transplant in South Africa in December 1967, I produced several large clay sculptures loosely based on that momentous event. I referred to these as my Transplant Series.

Porcelain

When I obtained a supply of porcelain clay from England, I was faced with a new challenge and new opportunities. Porcelain clay has two important qualities. One: it's strong and it holds its shape well. Two: when vitrified, it becomes translucent, particularly in thin section. To take maximum advantage of these characteristics, I made a series of small, narrow vases. Some of these were pinched or twisted into interesting shapes and to others, I added flanges. I also formed some delicate small bowls with irregular rims and in one of these, I placed a small figure of a kneeling woman. However, even the convention of using porcelain for delicate objects can be broken as I proved by making some solid sculptural objects from this material.

---

[6] Daniel Rhodes, ***Clay and Glazes for the Potter,*** Martino Fine Books, England, 1957.

Decorative tiles

In addition to thrown and hand-built forms, I experimented with a series of hand-made, glazed textured tiles, each about 400 mm x 200 mm, which were assembled in panels to be mounted on both exterior and interior walls. Some were adhered directly to walls, while others were mounted on a horizontal plywood base usually between 1.5 metres and 2 metres long.

The Group

In the years between the WW I and WW II an attitude arose among a number of young and talented artists, in protest against the long-established conventions of art-society selection processes. They argued that the old-fashioned, traditional 'rules' no longer applied and that the time had come to experiment with new techniques and ideas. An entity was established and named simply "The Group". The members were mostly full-time artists from Christchurch, but also included some leading practitioners from other centres. Initially, the majority of members were painters and printmakers, but later they included craftspeople with outstanding work, including sculptors, a woodworker, a weaver, and two potters.

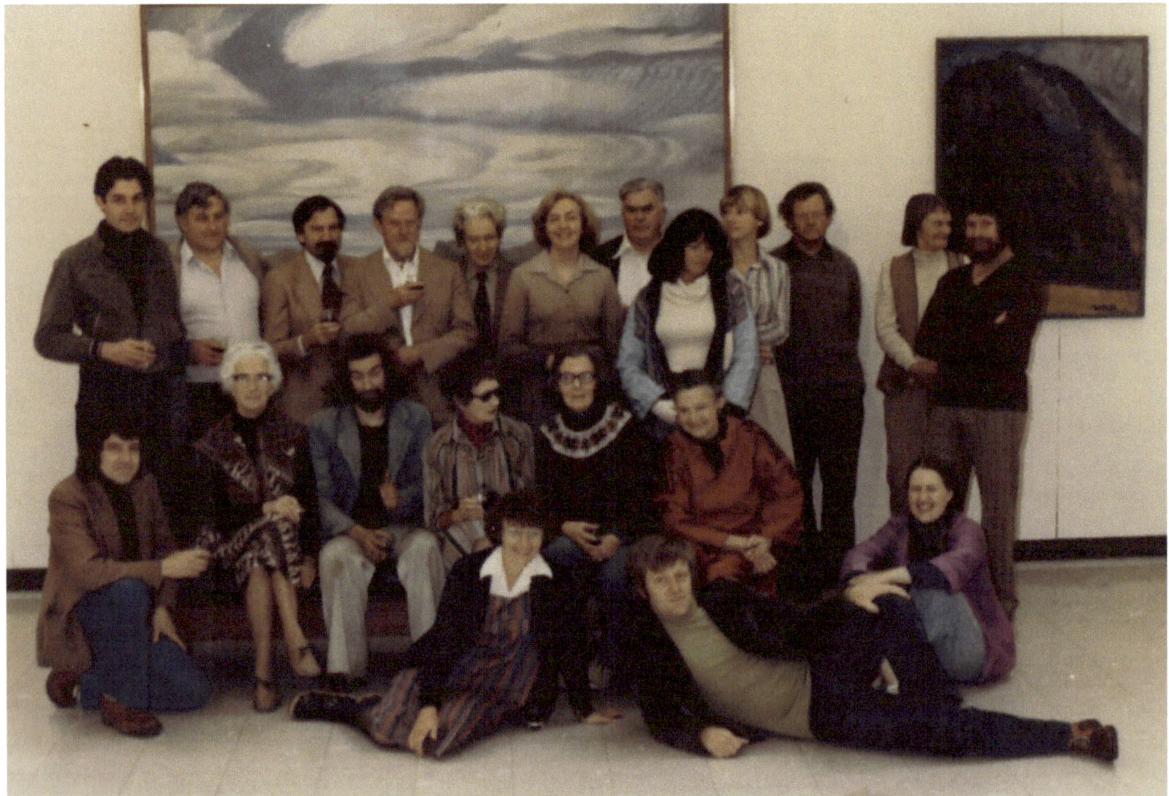

Some of the 'Group' members, CSA Gallery, Christchurch, 1977.
From left, standing: Gavin Bishop, Trevor Moffitt, John Coley, Bill Sutton, Pat Mulcahy, Nola Barron, Leo Bensemann, Rosemary Campbell, Vivien Bishop, Toss Woollaston, Juliet Peter, John Turner. Seated: Ida Lough, Philip Clairmont, Doris Lusk, Ria Bancroft, Olivia Spencer Bower. Front: Quentin MacFarlane, Jenny Hunt, Tom Field, Rosemary Johnson.
Photo: Owen Barron

The Group's first 'rule' was that there should be no rules. There was no committee, no chairman or leader, no written agenda, and no minutes of meetings etc. Members met twice a year, usually in a local hostelry, to discuss and make decisions on only two matters: to arrange the annual Group show and to invite talented artists to membership.

Matters were debated, sometimes forcefully, and eventually agreed to by consensus. In spite of this seeming lack of formality, the Group show was one of the highlights of the arts calendar. The standard of work shown at these exhibitions was exceptionally high. Openings were well attended, and sales indicated a genuine interest from buyers both private and institutional. I was invited to join the Group in 1967 and continued to exhibit with it until it was disbanded in 1977.

A new studio

In 1969 we moved from Shirley to Heaton Street in central Christchurch. With neighbouring properties close by it was not practical to have an oil-fired kiln, so I purchased a kiln that was fired with LPG (liquid petroleum gas). The gas kiln was never as satisfying as the old oil-fired one and, for a few months, my potting friend David Brokenshire kindly fired a number of my pieces in his kiln. I worked initially in a downstairs room of our home until we built a studio and workshop on the back boundary. About this time, my interest changed from pottery to sculpture and I exchanged working with clay to grinding and polishing bronze.

Pottery collection

Over the years, I established a collection of work by some of New Zealand's leading potters. Sadly, most of this collection, along with many of my own work, was destroyed in the severe earthquake which struck Christchurch on February 22, 2011.

Sales

At that time the few specialist art dealers were not interested in including pottery in their exhibitions. Some retailers stocked pottery, but it was mainly small domestic work with a limited range of colours. Small quantities of earthenware pottery were being produced by early potters using commercial coloured glazes imported from England. Like watercolour painting, earthenware is a fiendishly difficult medium to work in to produce satisfactory results. By the late 1950s, there were a few professional, full-time potters making a living from their craft. Some were recent immigrants who had worked as potters in their home country and some were New Zealanders who had discovered an affinity with clay as a medium for their creativity. They often sold their work from a room adjacent to their workshop.

In the 1960s and 1970s, art shops and small galleries began to include pottery and other crafts, along with painting, prints and other visual arts, in their stock. I sold some of my work through the following outlets:

- Little Woodwork Shop in Victoria Street, Christchurch. Owned by Joe White.

- Guenter Taemmler's jewellery shop in Merivale, Christchurch.

- General Trading Company in Cashel Street, Christchurch.

- Several Arts, in Colombo Street, North, Christchurch, owned by Michael and Victoria Trumic, and George Kojis, and later by Ngaire Hewson.

- Kees Groenendaal's Design Shop in Manchester Street, Christchurch.

- Cave Rock Gallery, owned by Noeline Brokenshire. Initially in Sumner and later at The Arts Centre, Christchurch
- Studio 393, Montreal Street, Christchurch, owned by a collective of Christchurch potters.
- Décor Gallery, Timaru.
- Alicat in Auckland, owned by television personality Peter Sinclair
- The Colonial Gallery, in Timaru, owned by Nora Garland.

Examples of my work were accepted for each of the annual exhibitions of the New Zealand Society of Potters from 1964 to 1986. I also showed pottery in annual exhibitions of both the Canterbury Potters Association and the CSA; the New Zealand Academy of Fine Arts, Wellington, and in several other shows and exhibitions locally and nationally. My pottery was well received by both the public and art critics. The demand for hand-made pottery was such that at every exhibition people formed a queue to place red stickers on their chosen articles and most of the Exhibited were sold within minutes of the show opening.

Some of my pottery was purchased by the following public institutions:

- Robert McDougall Art Gallery, now Christchurch Art Gallery Te Puna o Waiwhetū
- Canterbury Museum
- Christchurch Teachers' Training College (work transferred to University of Canterbury), and
- Canterbury Potters Association.

A ceramic form, 'Landscape Rhythm' (1972), was purchased by the Ministry of Foreign Affairs and Trade for display in a New Zealand Embassy overseas. The Bank of New Zealand bought another piece for its office in New York. Several of my decorative wall panels went to private collectors, including fellow artist Doris Lusk and the owner of Shades Station in Marlborough. A panel of tiles entitled 'First Snow' (1979) was bought by a corporate business, Lombard New Zealand Ltd, in Wellington and displayed in the entrance foyer of its building until its demise. Another work, 'Maisie Hill Memorial Ceramic Panel' (1969), decorates the administrative wing of Christchurch Girls' High School, where I was a student from 1944 to 1948.

Summary

Section One deals with the establishment of the craft of pottery in New Zealand and my own involvement: my training as a potter and the setting-up of my own studio and kiln. The practice of studio pottery was still in its early stages and there was little tuition available. Early enthusiasts learned by trial and error, and information was shared generously.

I employed several techniques to achieve my desired results. Beginning with traditional domestic pottery thrown on a kick-wheel and then, as interest developed into more sculptural forms, adopting a hand-made method known as coiling, which enabled me to make objects up to 60 or 70 centimetres high. Freed from the restraints of making my living from pottery, I was able to experiment with clay to produce sculptural forms for my own satisfaction. I used stoneware clay fired to 1300 degrees centigrade for all my work. For larger sculptural shapes I usually relied on a plain white glaze with no decoration as I wished to emphasise the form. With English porcelain clay I was able to produce shapes that would not have been possible in ordinary clay. I also made several tile panels. These became decorative features in homes and commercial buildings, both internally and externally.

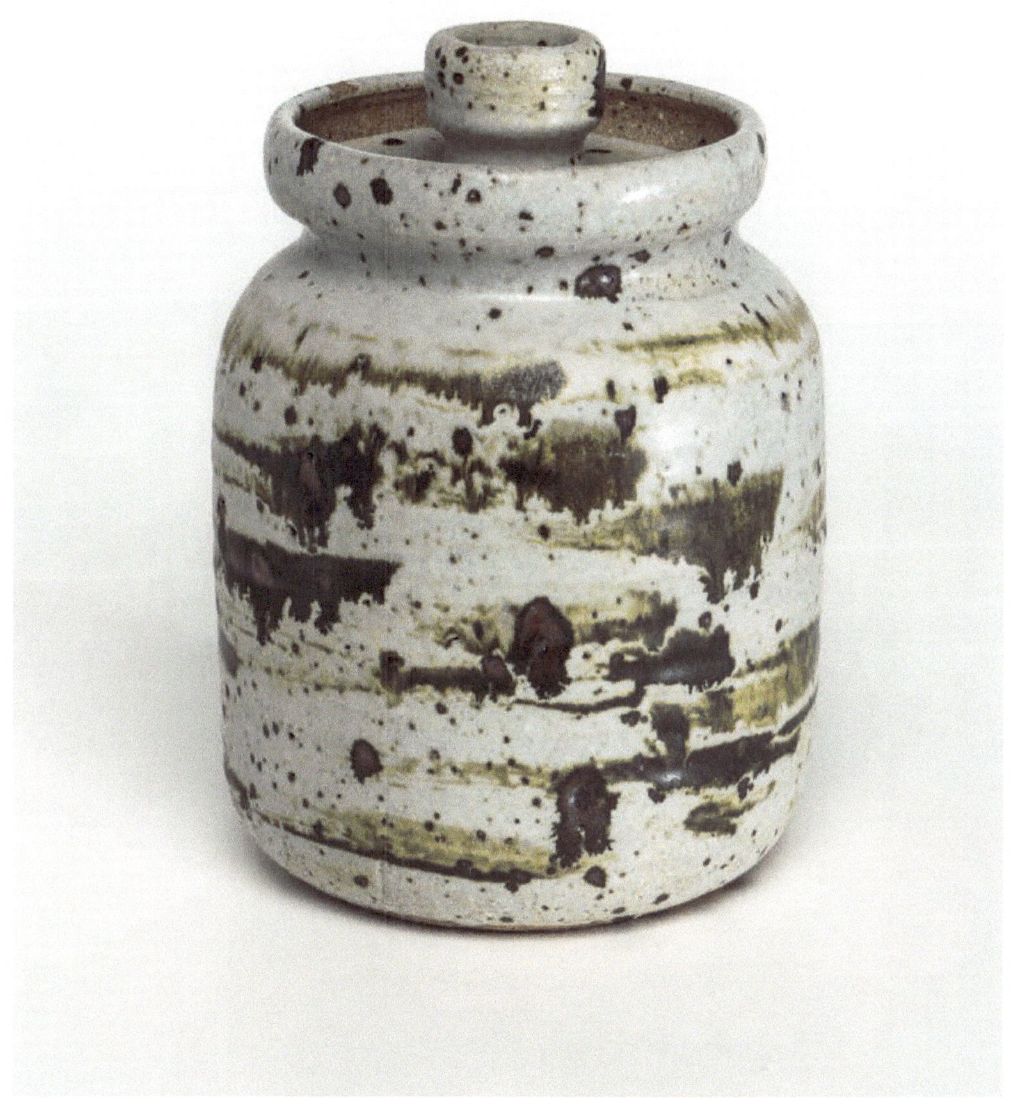

Lidded Jar c 1967
stoneware
h 198 w 140 mm
impressed mark
Collection of the artist
Photo: John Collie

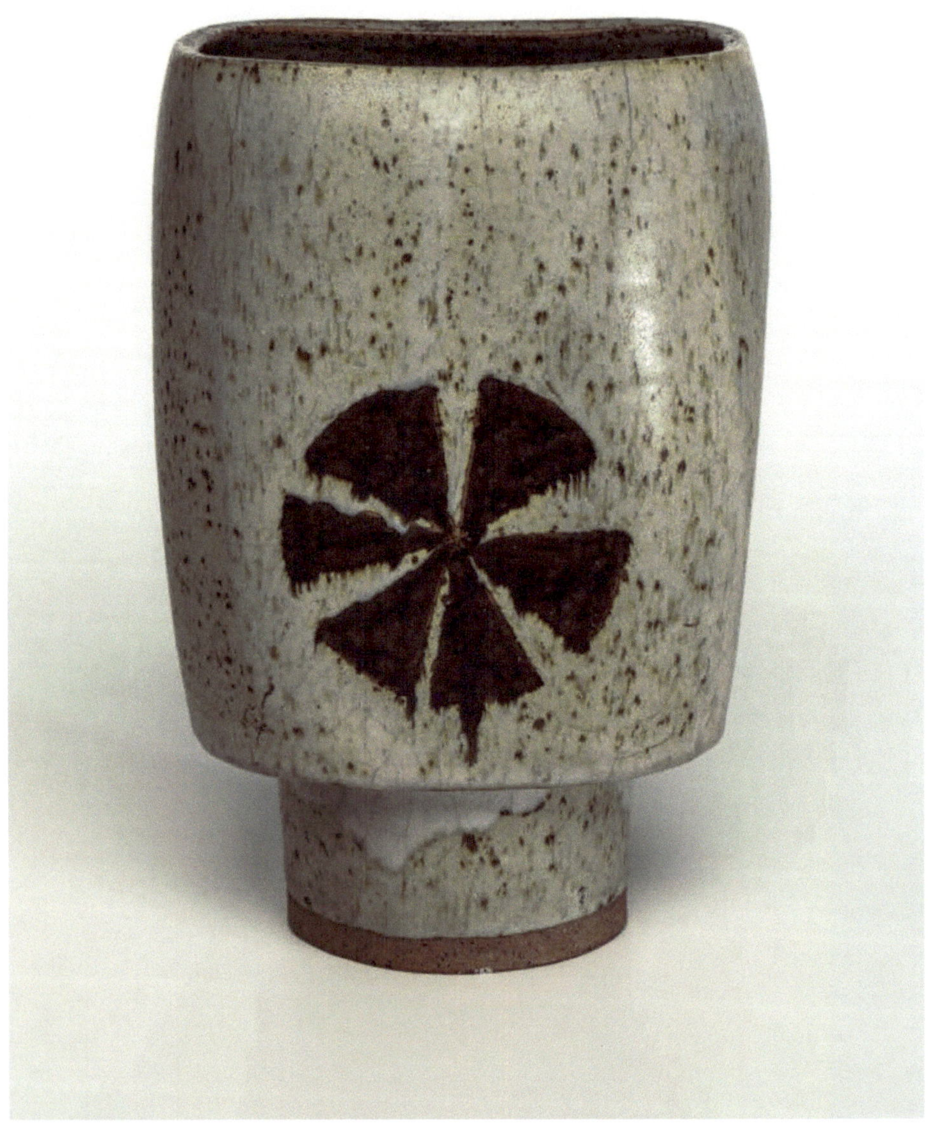

Pot c 1967
stoneware
250 x 165 x 140 mm
impressed mark
Collection of the artist
Photo: John Collie

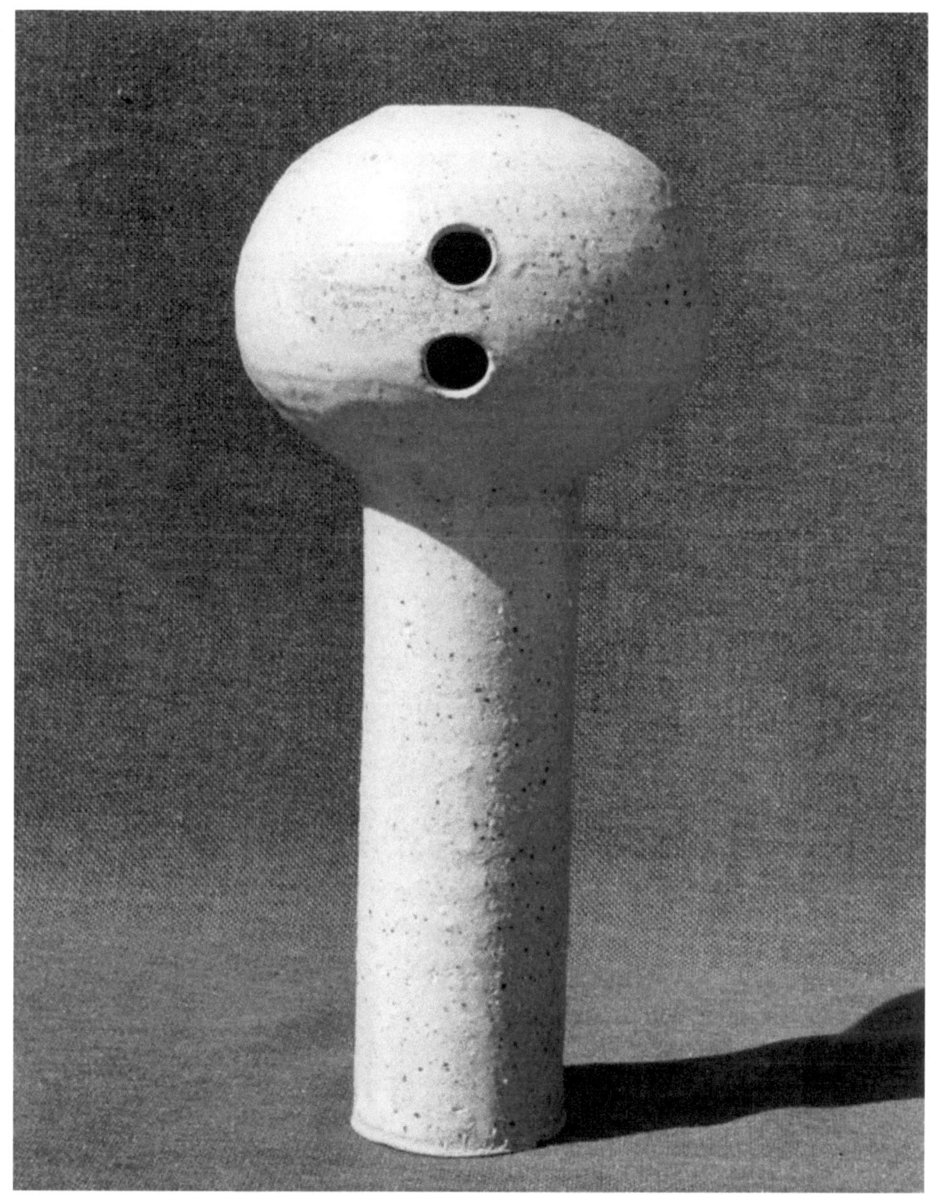

People pot c 1967
Stoneware
h 325 mm (approx)
whereabouts unknown
Photo Nola Barron Archives

Note
Three 'People Pots' were exhibited in 1967 New Zealand Society of Potters 11th Exhibition, Display Centre, Palmerston North.
Reference: illustration in ***New Zealand Potter***, Volume 10, Number 1, March 1968, p. 11.

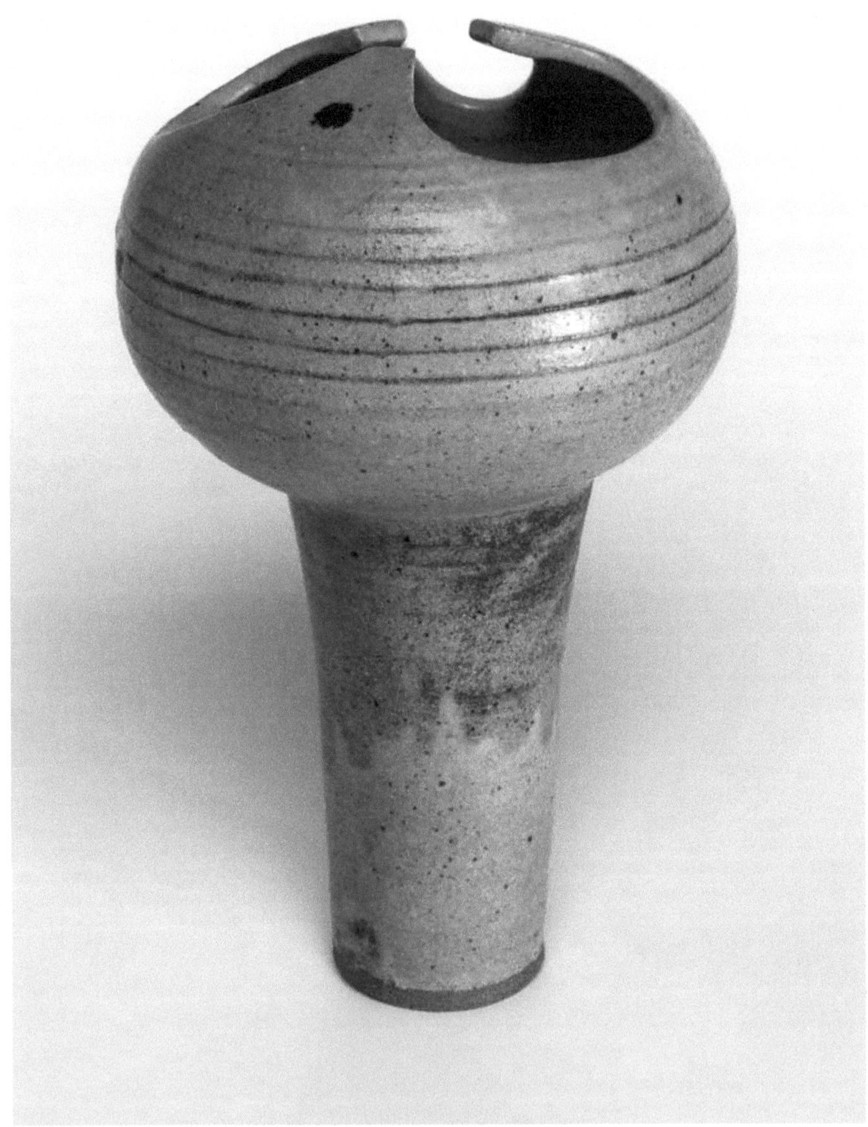

People pot 'Mouth' c 1968
stoneware
h 288 mm w 165 mm
impressed mark
Collection of the artist
Photo: John Collie

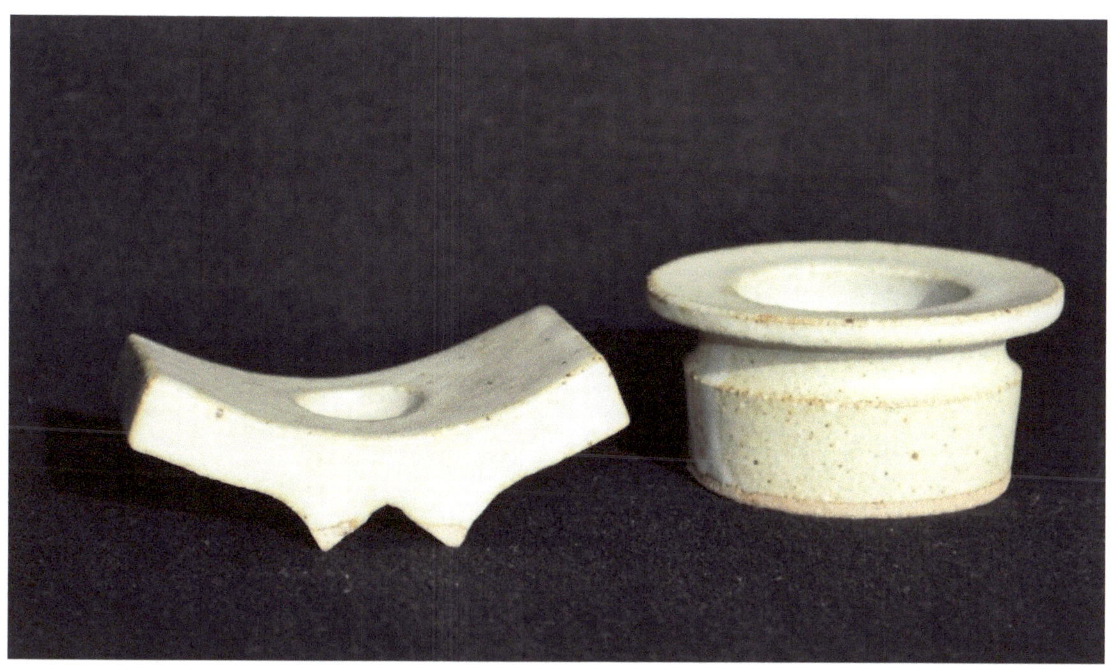

Two Candleholders c 1960s
stoneware

Left
h 40 x 105 x 45 mm (approx)
Collection of the artsist

Right
h 50 mm w 100 mm
impressed mark inscribed '862'
Collection of the artist
Photo: Nola Barron Archives

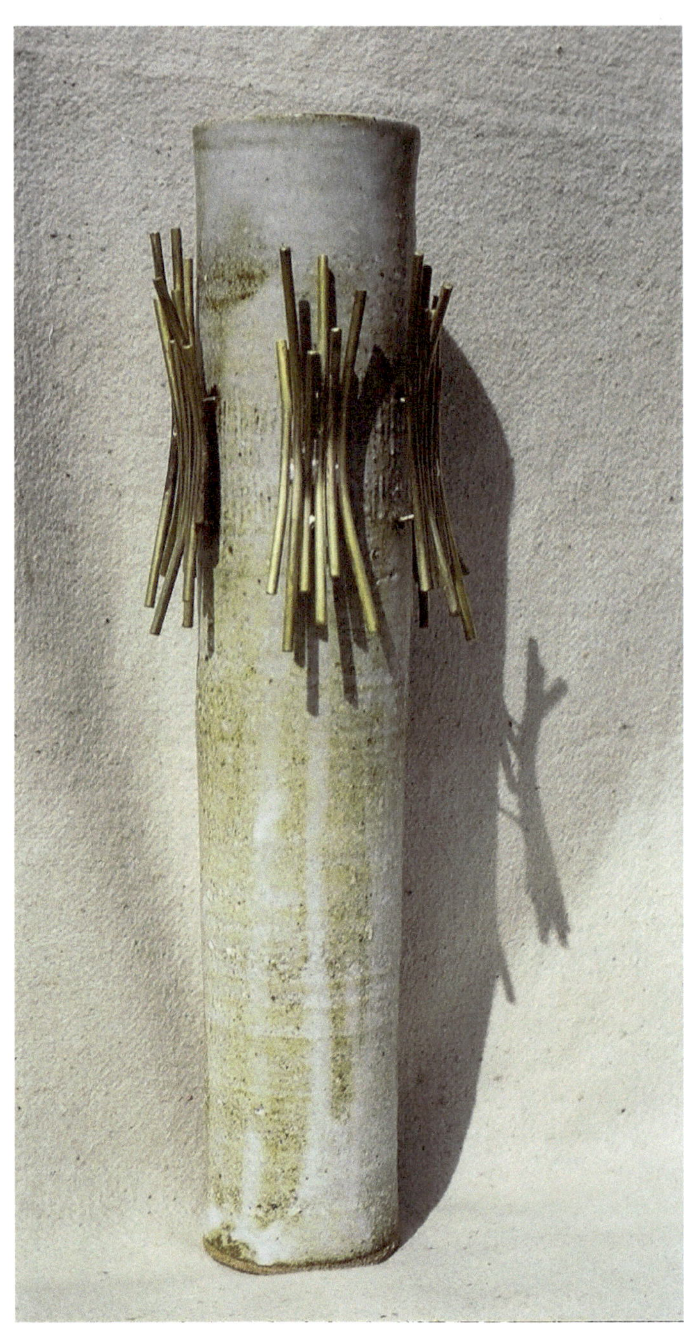

Vase 1969
stoneware, brass wire
h 342 mm w 100 mm
impressed mark, inscribed 580
Collection of the artist
Photo: Nola Barron Archives

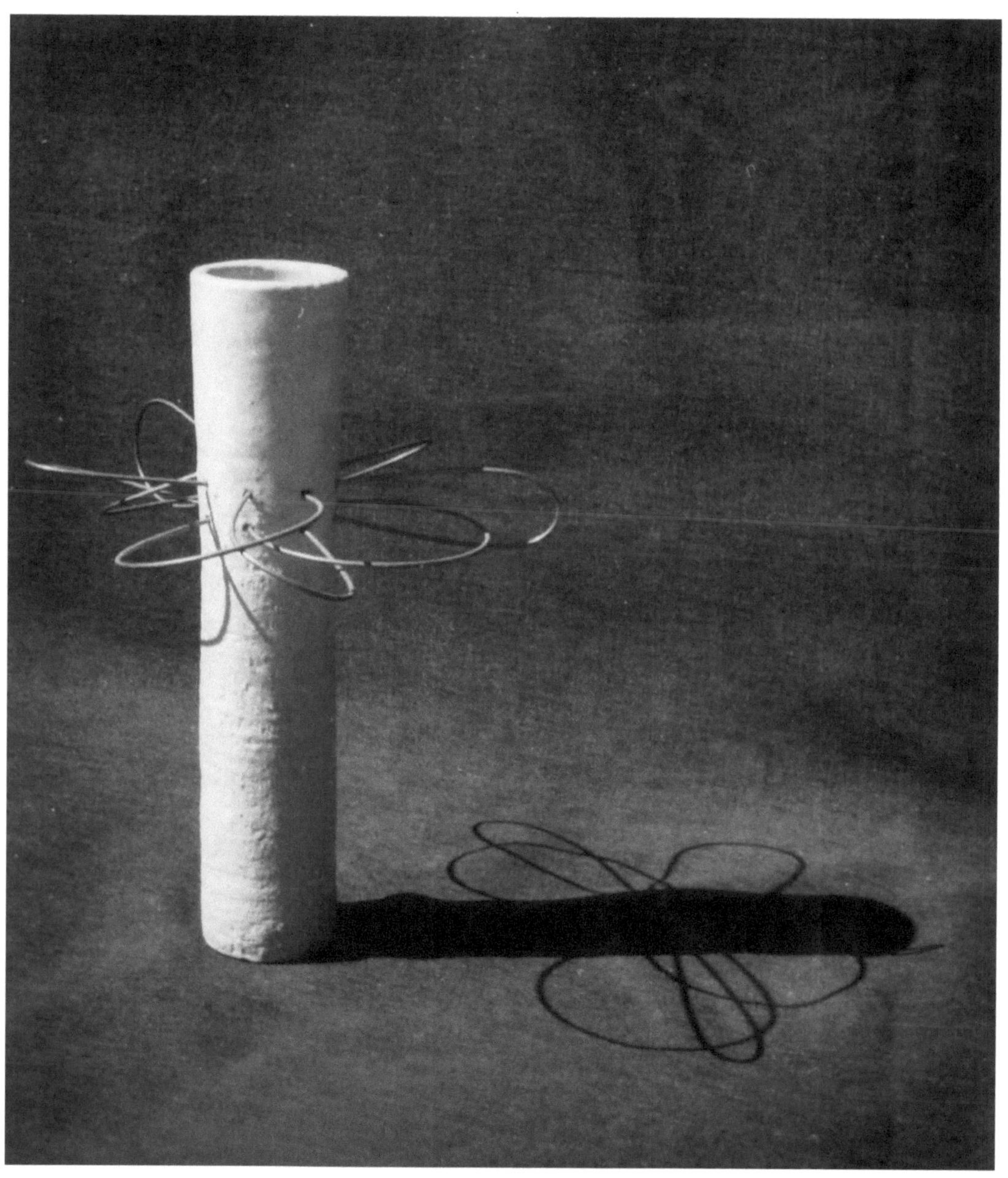

Orbit 1969
stoneware, brass wire
h 330 mm w 290 mm
impressed mark, inscribed 575
Collection of the artist
Photo: Robert Prisk, Nola Barron Archives

Reference
Illustrated in **New Zealand Potter**, Volume II, Number I, Autumn 1969. p. 28.

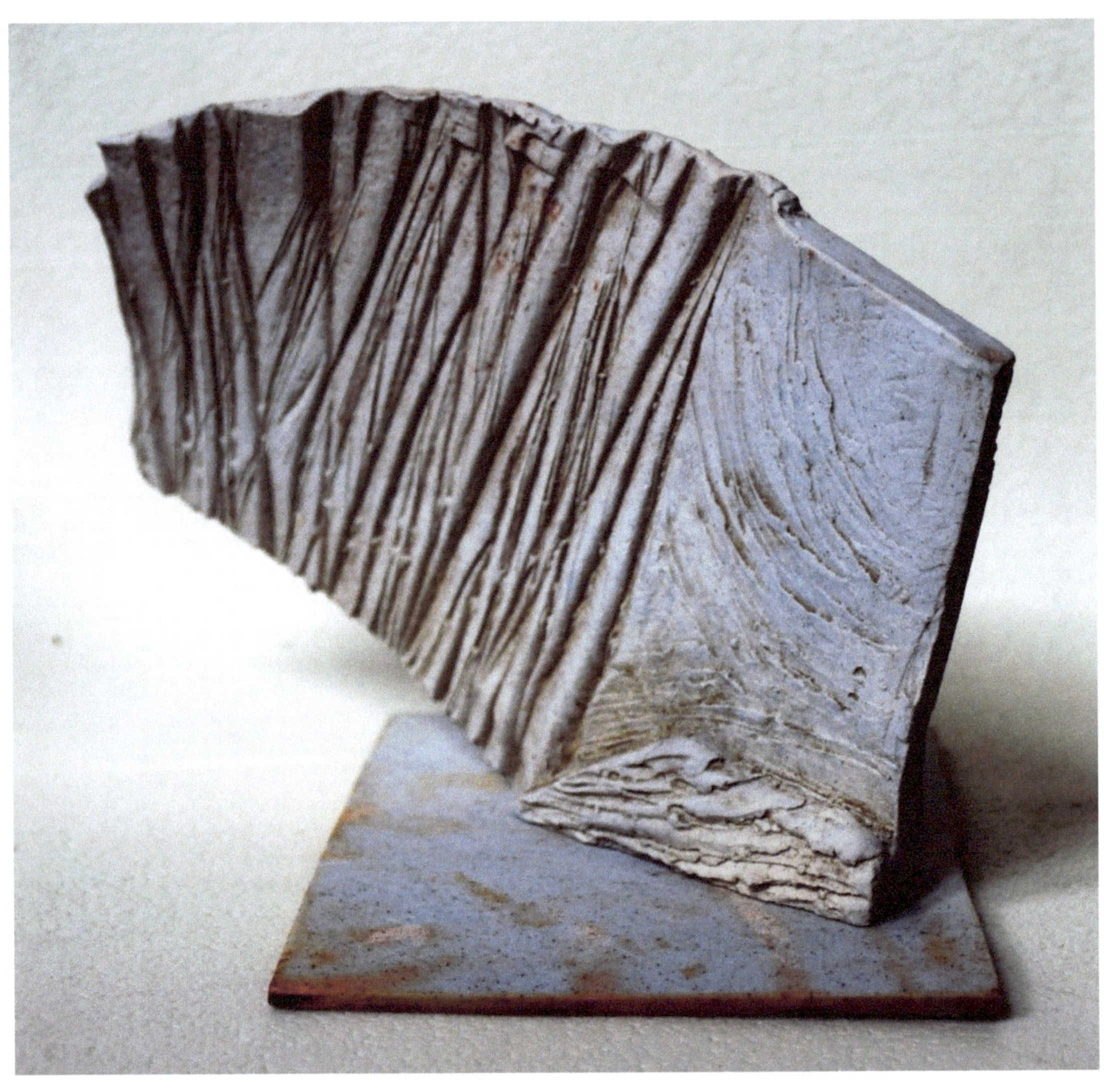

Wind & Rain 1977
stoneware
h 250 mm (approx)
whereabouts unknown
Photo: Nola Barron Archives

Exhibited
1977 Canterbury Society of Arts Craft Exhibition: Fine Crafts Woven Hangings Decorative &
Sculptural Ceramics, CSA Gallery, Christchurch, cat. 1.

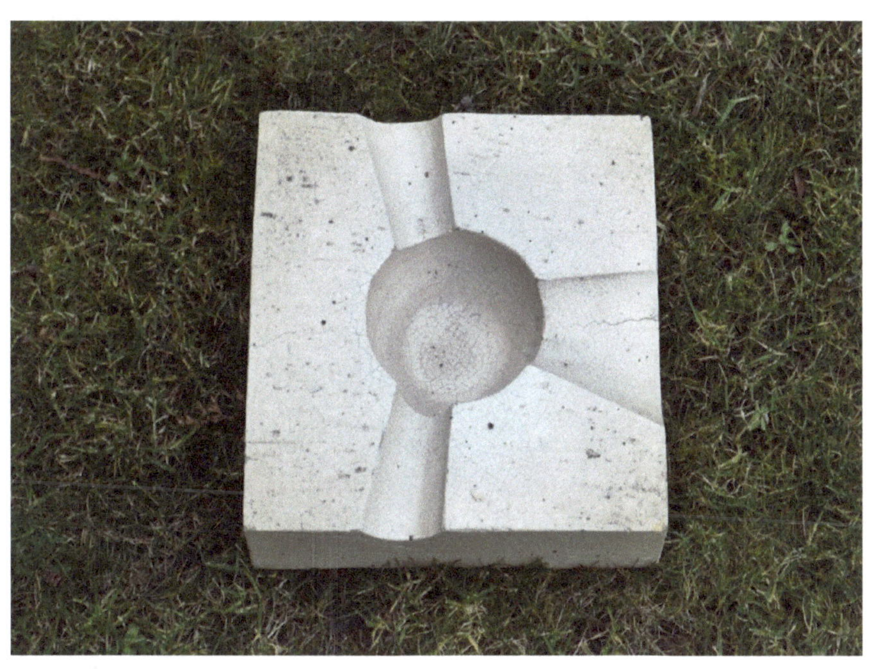

Ashtray c 1967
stoneware
h 60 mm w 230 mm
impressed mark, inscribed 2036
Collection of the artist
Photo: Owen Barron

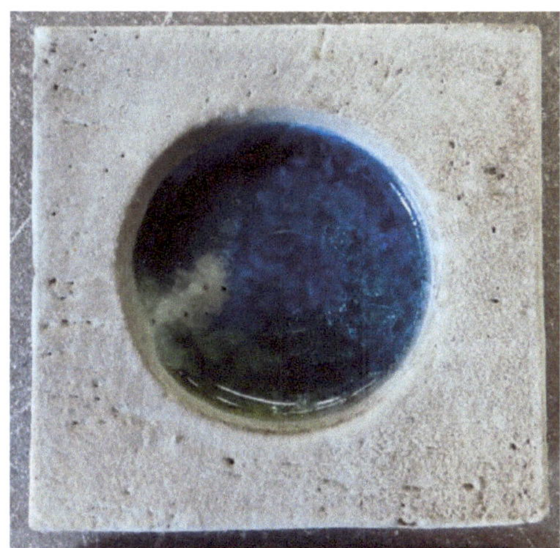

Ashtray c 1974
Stoneware, glass
inscribed 2359
30 x 112 x 112 mm
Collection of Canterbury Potters'
Association
Photo: Grant Banbury

Note: Six ashtrays were included in the
Zonta Club of Christchurch: First
Exhibition of Pottery & Painting, 1974,
The Capricorn Gallery, Christchurch.

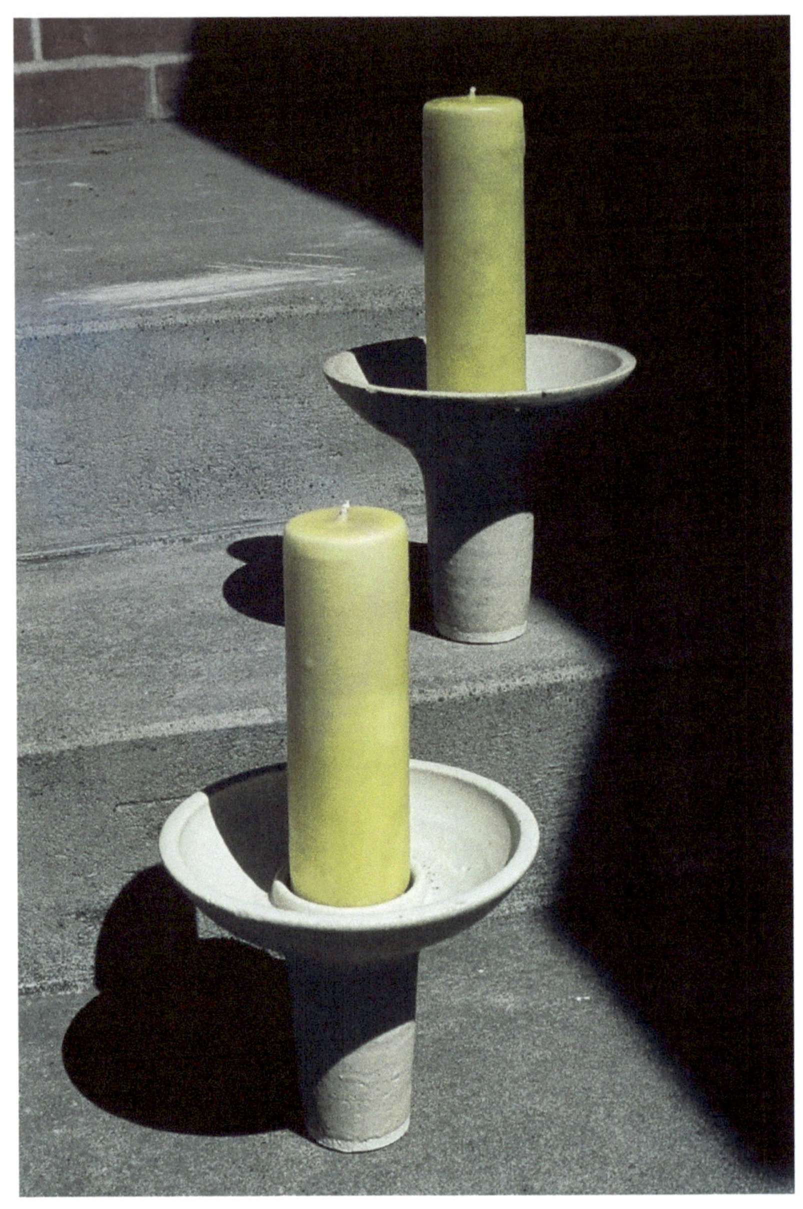

Pair of Candleholders 1969
stoneware
h 156 x w 175 mm (each)
impressed mark
Photo: Nola Barron Archives

Exhibited
1969 New Zealand Society of Potters 13th National Exhibition, Auckland War Memorial Museum,
cat 4. as 'Pair Candleholders and candles'.
Top Collection of Grant Banbury.

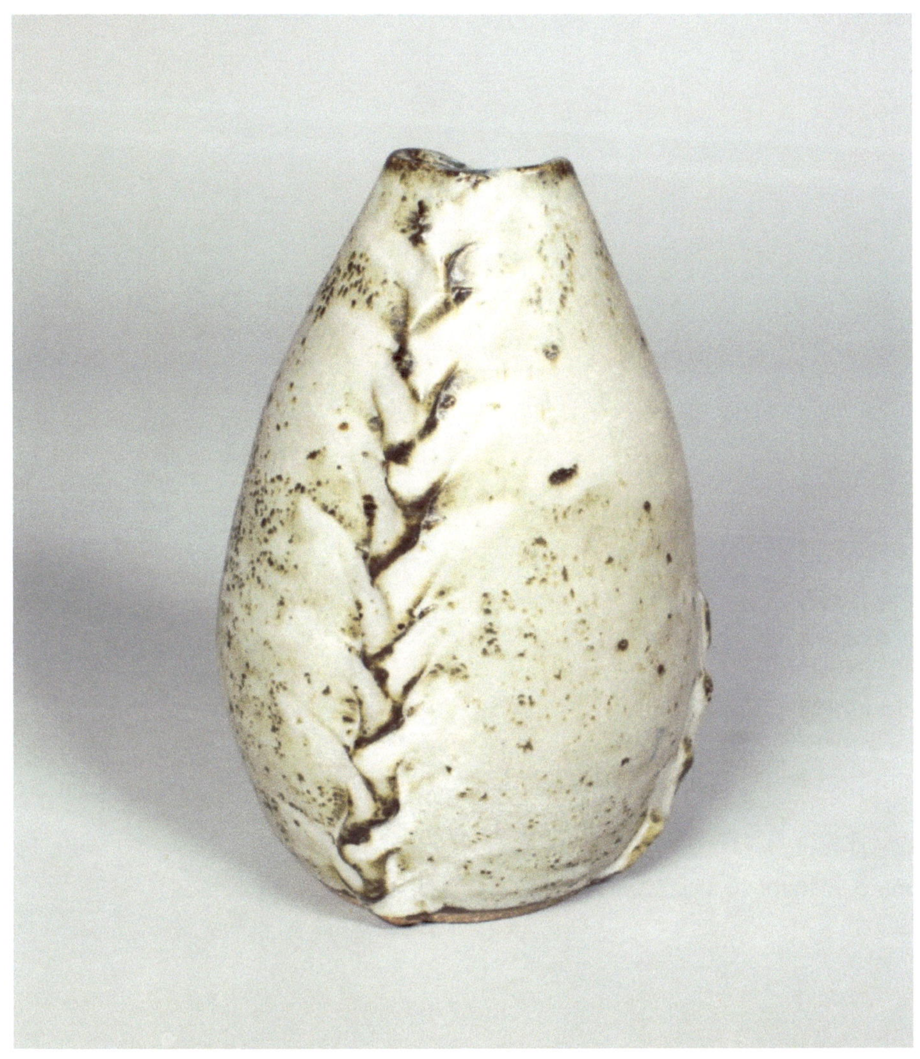

Ear of wheat 1966
stoneware
h 338 x w 163 mm
Impressed mark, original exhibition label N. Barron 3.3.0, label 17
Canterbury Museum Collection C.1966.47
Photo: Canterbury Museum

Exhibited
1966 New Zealand Society of Potters 10th National Exhibition, Christchurch, cat 17 as
'Vase'

Reference
Illustrated Moyra Elliott and Damien Skinner, Cone Ten Down: Studio Pottery in New
Zealand, 1945-1980, David Bateman, 2009, p.133.

Sculptural Form 1967

oil fired stoneware
h 338 mm w 163 mm
impressed mark, inscribed 780
Purchased by Robert McDougall
Art Gallery 1971
Collection Christchurch Art
Gallery Te Puna o Waiwhetu
71/13
Photo: John Collie

Exhibited
1988-9 Canterbury Potters
Association 25th Anniversary
Retrospective Exhibition,
Robert McDougall Art
Gallery, Christchurch, cat 5.

Reference
Illustrated *New Zealand Potter*, Volume 11, Number 1, Autumn 1969, p. 29.
See exhibition installation photograph of Canterbury Potters Association 25th Retrospective
Exhibition, Robert
McDougall Art Gallery, *New Zealand Potter*, Volume 31, Number 1, 1989, p. 9.

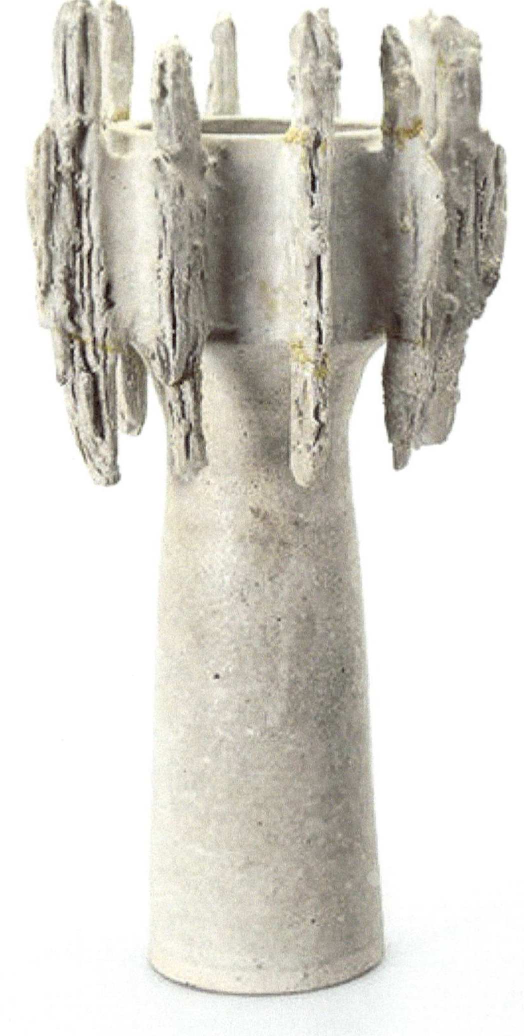

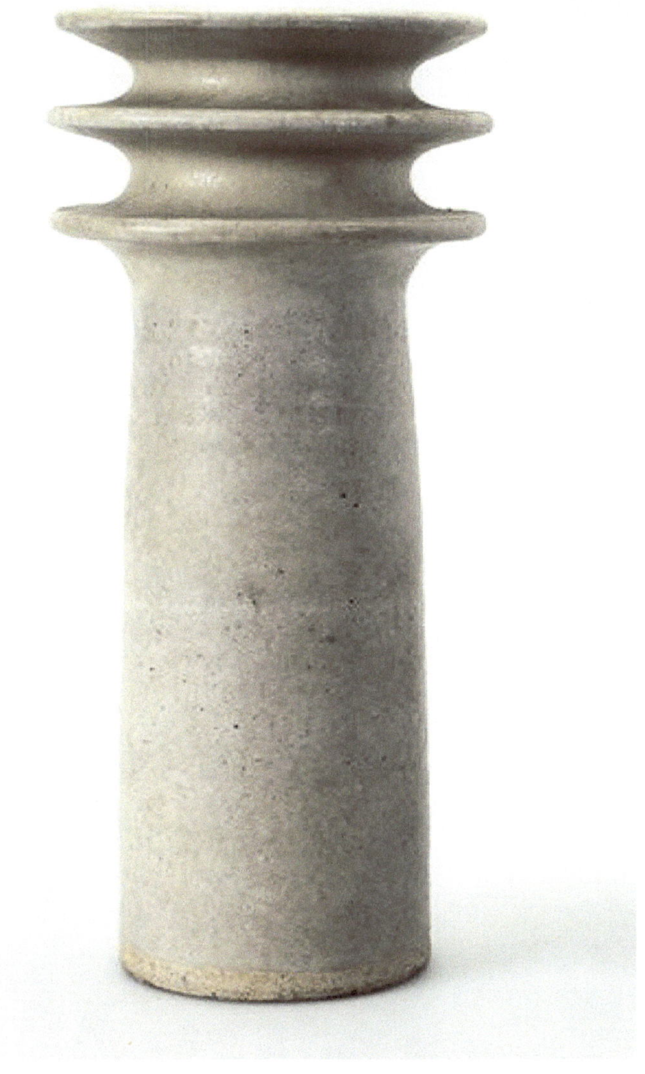

Candlestick 1969
oil fired stoneware
h 302 mm w 111 mm
impressed mark, inscribed 488
Purchased by Robert McDougall Art Gallery 1971
Collection Christchurch Art Gallery Te Puna o Waiwhetu 71/12
Photo: John Collie

Exhibited
1969 New Zealand Society of Potters 13th National Exhibition, CSA Gallery, Christchurch, cat 5.
2016 '1969 Comeback Special', Christchurch Art Gallery Te Puna o Waiwhetū.

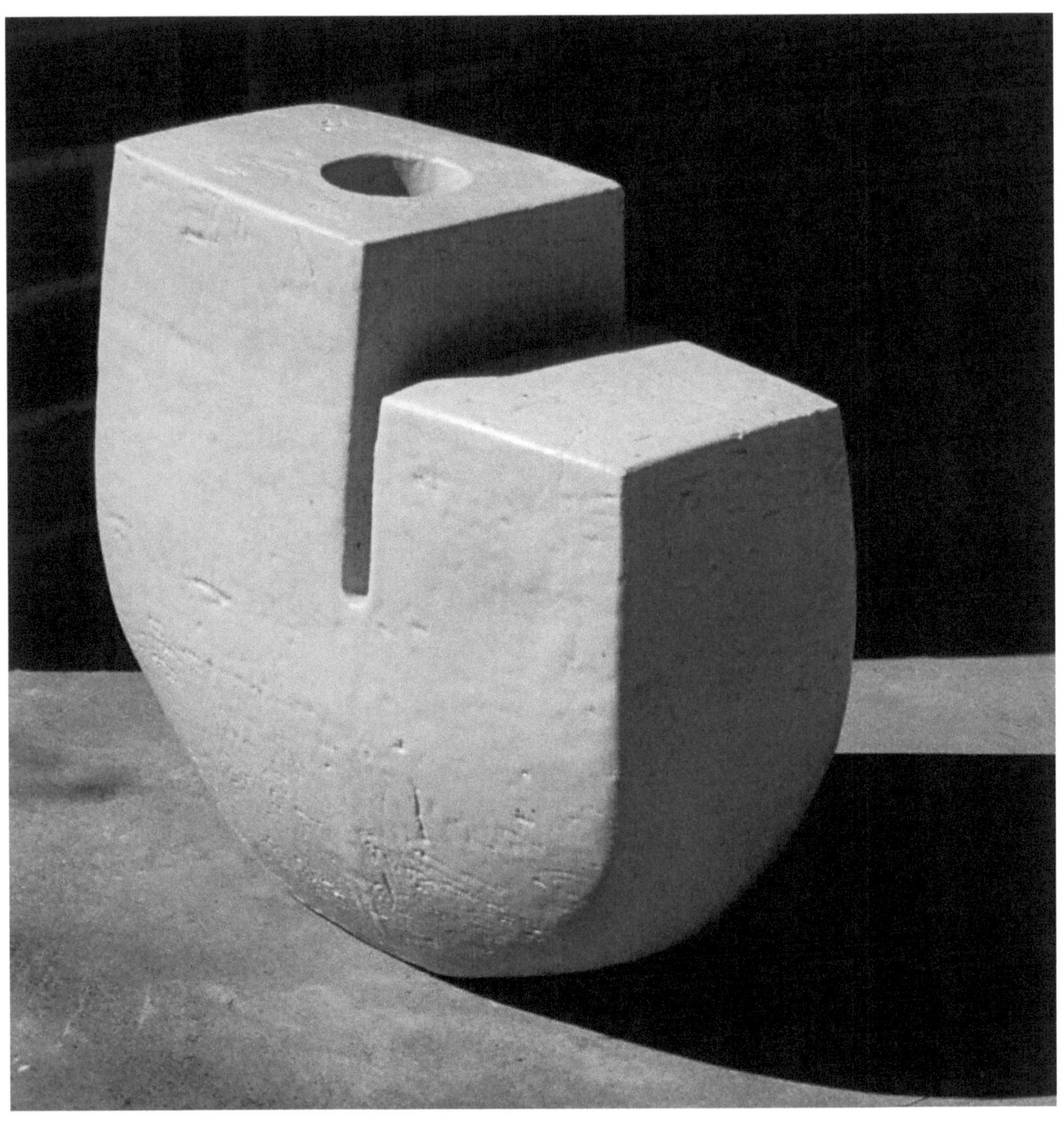

Ceramic Form 1970
stoneware
h 350 mm (approx)
whereabouts unknown
Photo: Nola Barron Archives

Exhibited 1970 'Invited Potters', Manawatu Art Gallery, Palmerston North, cat 1.
Reference Illustrated in David Aitken, "Outstanding Potter Exhibition: Vessels from The Potters' Hands," Evening Standard [Palmerston North], 11 December 1970, p. 10.

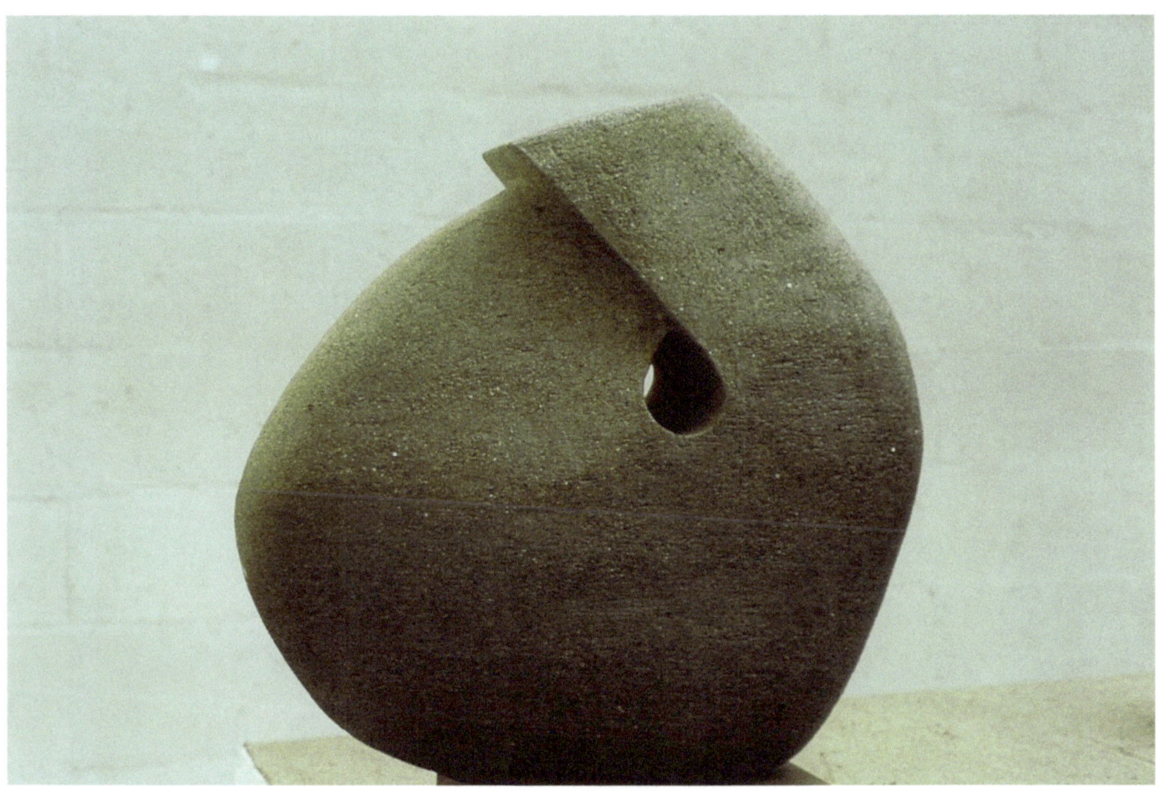

Coiled Ceramic Form 1971
stoneware - unglazed - attached to a wooden base
h 380 mm (approx)
inscribed 899
Photo: Nola Barron Archives

Exhibited
1971 New Zealand Society of Potters 14th National Exhibition, CSA Gallery, Christchurch, cat 29.
Purchased by Christchurch architect John Trengrove. Current whereabouts unknown.

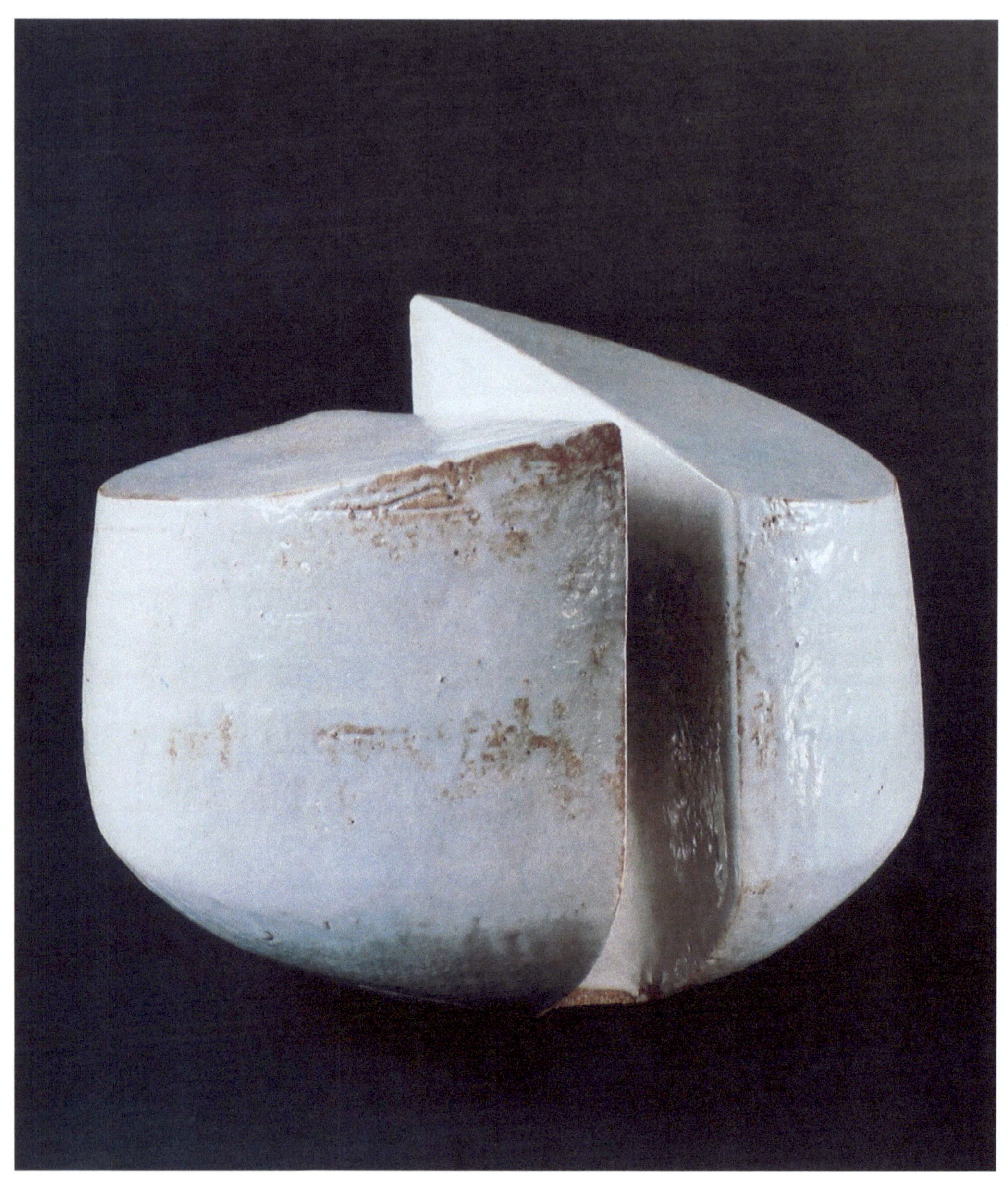

Double Split Form
undated, stoneware, h 190 mm w 240 mm
whereabouts unknown
Reproduction from Doreen Blumhardt & Brian Brake, Craft New Zealand: The art of the craftsman,
A.H. & A.W. Reed Ltd, 1981, p. 251.
Note: a work from this series was included in '1980 BNZ Art Award for Pottery Sculpture Print,' New
Zealand Academy of Fine Arts, Wellington as 'Sculptural Form'.

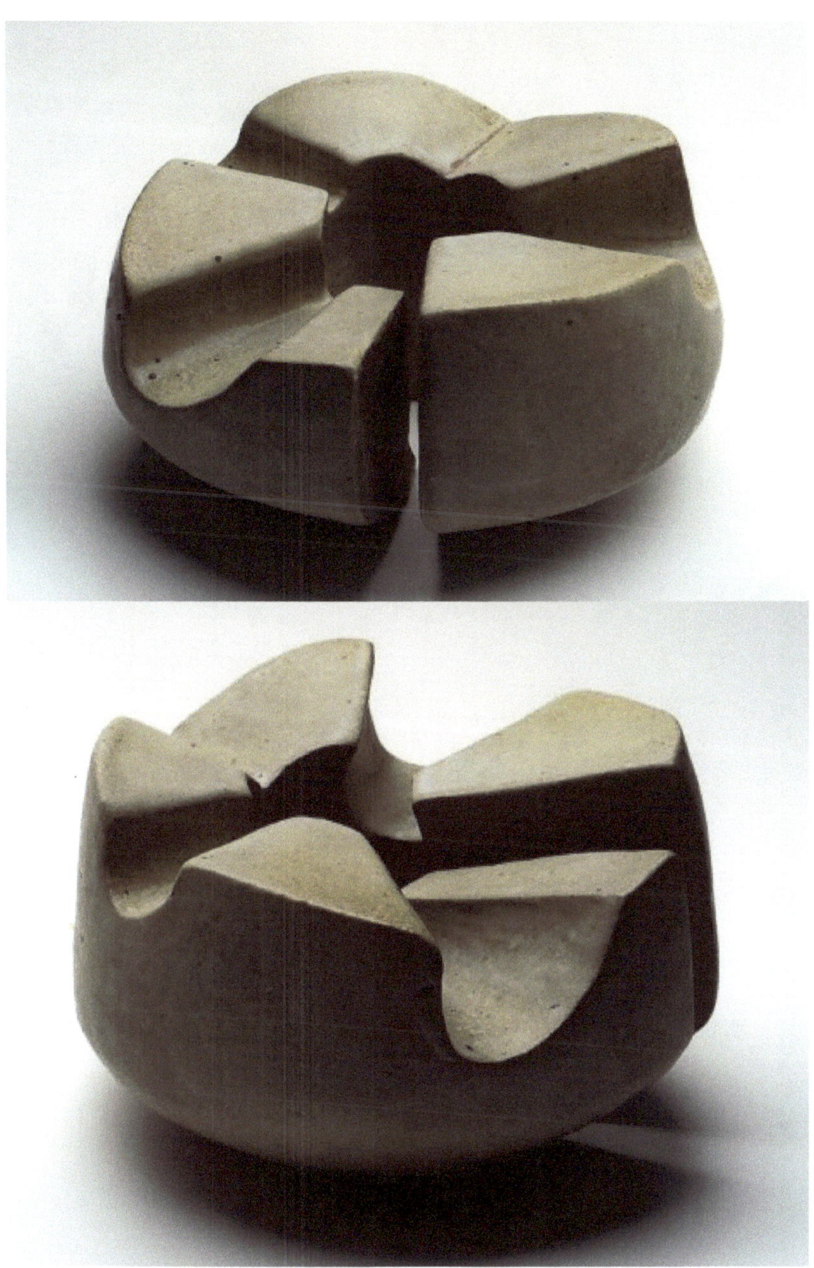

Ring Landform 1972
oil fired ceramic. h 140 w 217 mm. impressed mark, original label 1018
Collection Christchurch Art Gallery Te Puna o Waiwhetu 2007/004
Gifted by artist 2007. Photo: John Collie

Reference
Illustrated Peter Cape, Please Touch, A Survey of Three-Dimensional Arts in New Zealand, Collins, 1980, p. 100, as 'Landform'

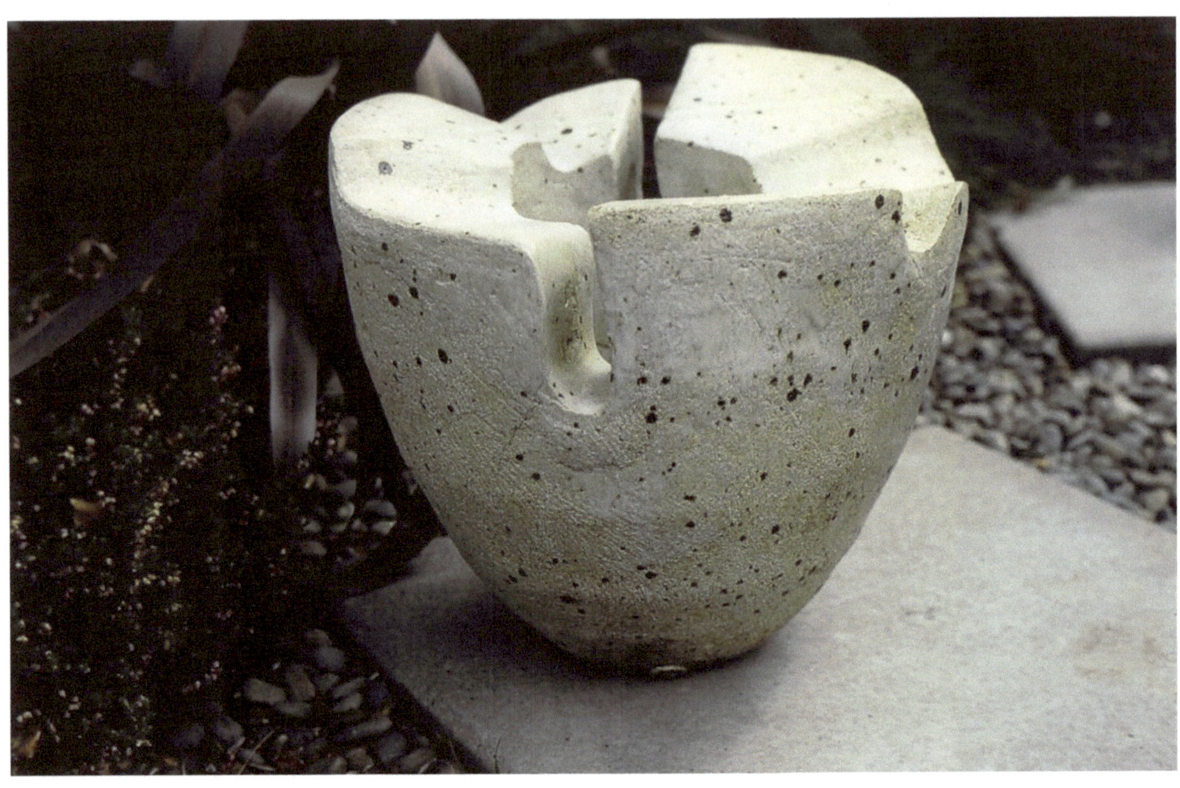

Ceramic Form I Landscape Rhythm 1972
stoneware
h 380 mm (approx)
inscribed 1074
Photo: Nola Barron Archives

Exhibited
1972 New Zealand Society of Potters 15th National Exhibition, New Zealand Academy of Fine Arts Gallery, Wellington, cat 29.

Purchased by Ministry of Foreign Affairs and Trade. Deaccessioned in 2008. Current whereabouts unknown.

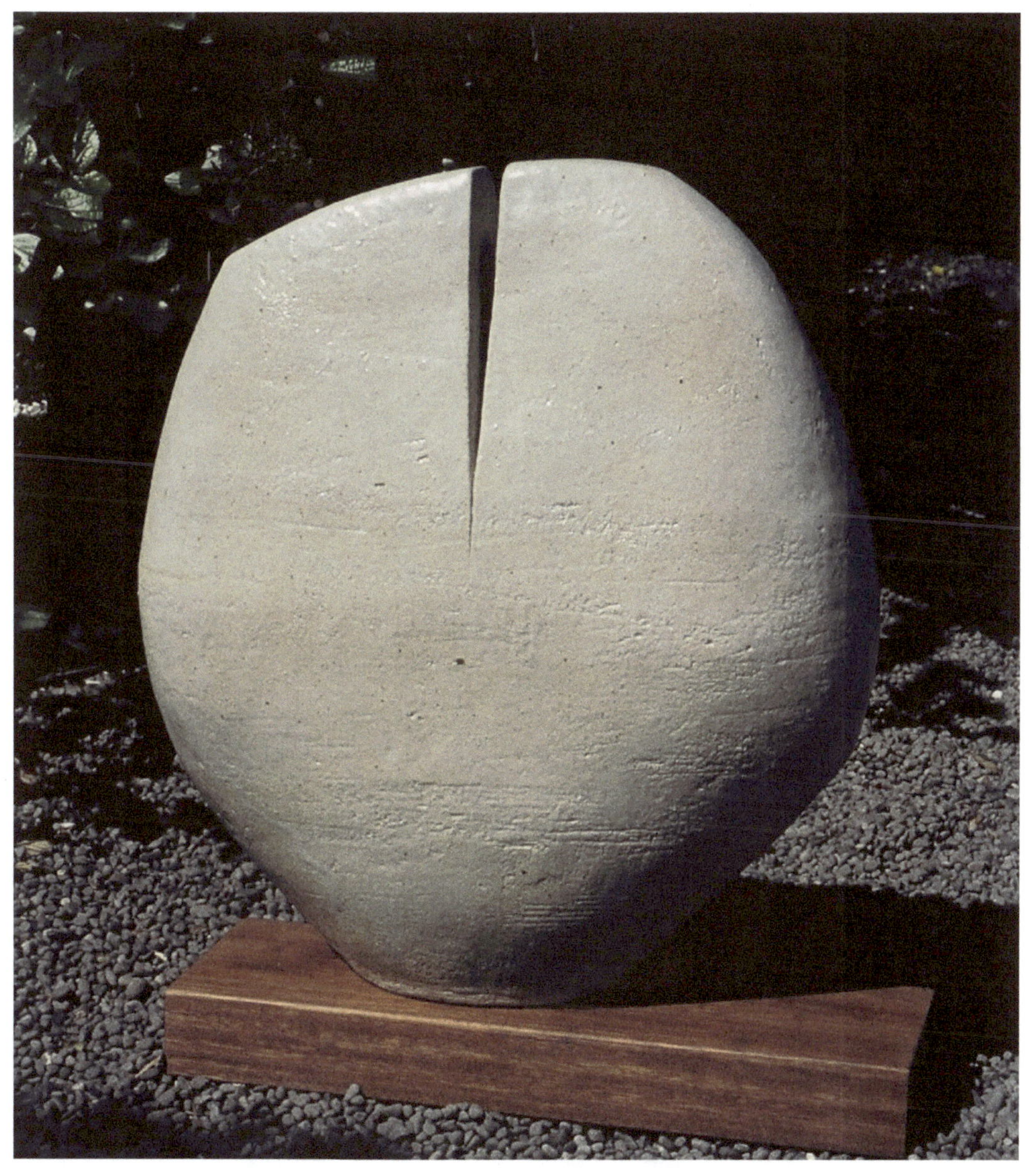

Opened Form 1969
Stoneware, wooden base - Rhodes 22 glaze. h 460 x 390 x 180 mm (approx)
Collection Quartz Museum, Whanganui. Formerly Simon Manchester collection.
Photo: Nola Barron Archives

Exhibited
New Zealand Society of Potters 13th National Exhibition, Auckland War Memorial Museum, cat 3.

Reference: Illustrated Denys Trussell, "Fire and Form", *NZ Listener*, August 12, 1978, p. 29.

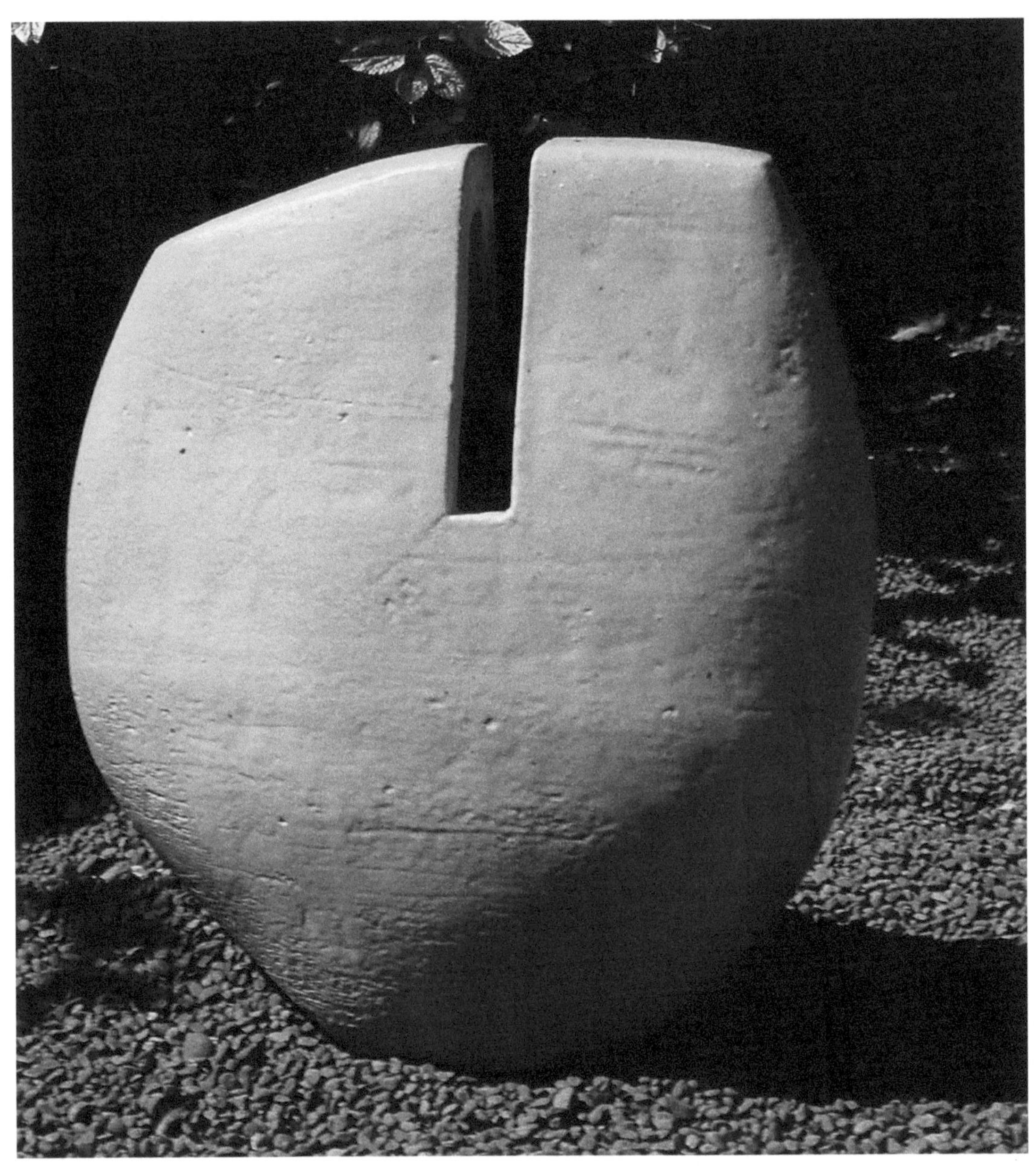

Large Split, 1969
stoneware - Rhodes glaze
460 x 390 x 180 mm
impressed mark
Collection of Rex Valentine, Christchurch. Formerly collection of Ida Lough, Christchurch.
Photo: Nola Barron archives

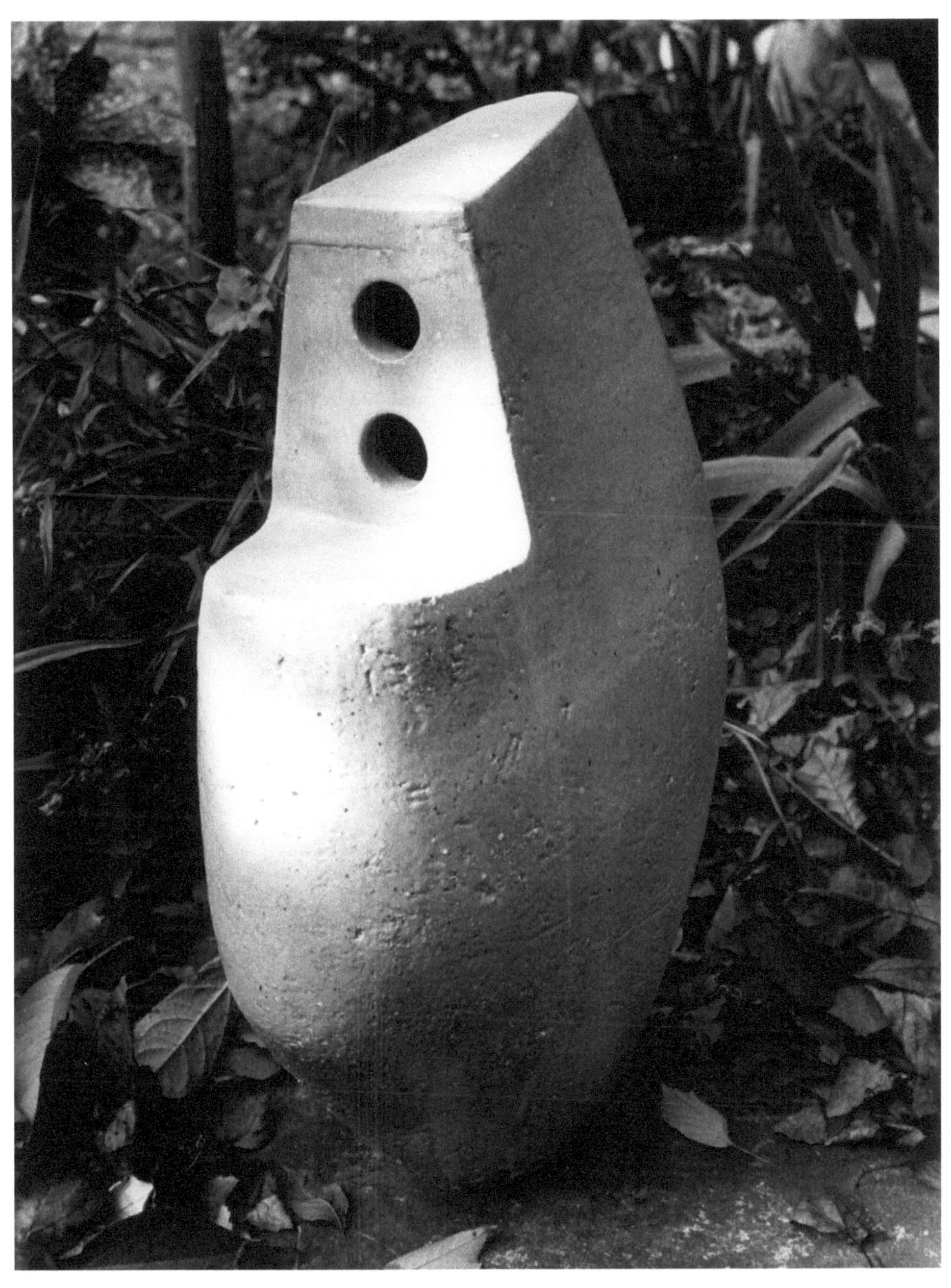

Form c 1969
stoneware - Rhodes glaze
h 520 mm w 380 mm
no inscription
Collection of the artist
Photo: Nola Barron Archives

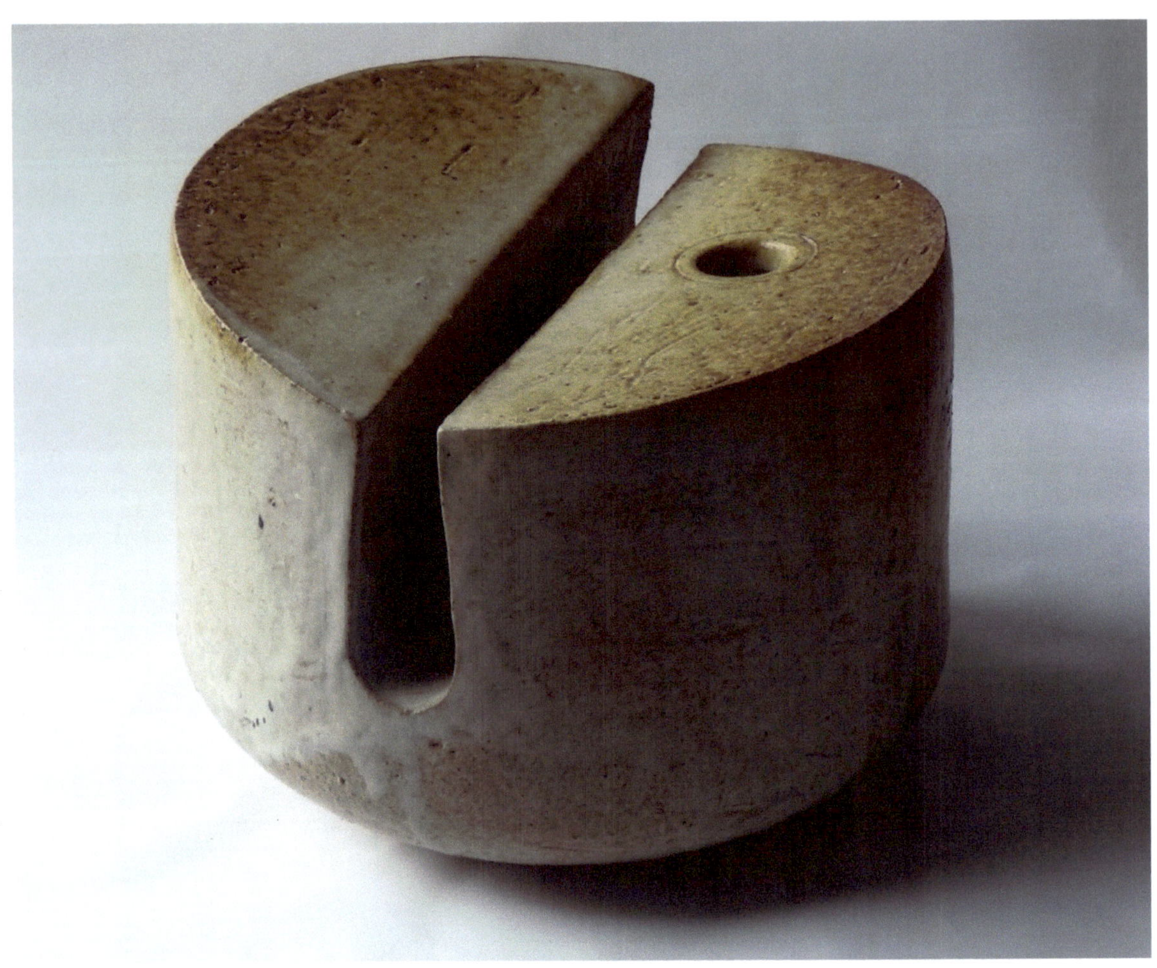

Landform 1971
stoneware
h 200 mm w 250 mm
impressed mark, incised Barron 71, 2327
Collection of Grant Banbury and Mark Hornby
Photo: Grant Banbury

Reference
Illustrated Moyra Elliott and Damien Skinner, Cone Ten Down: Studio Pottery in New Zealand, 1945-1980,
David Bateman 2009, p. 132.

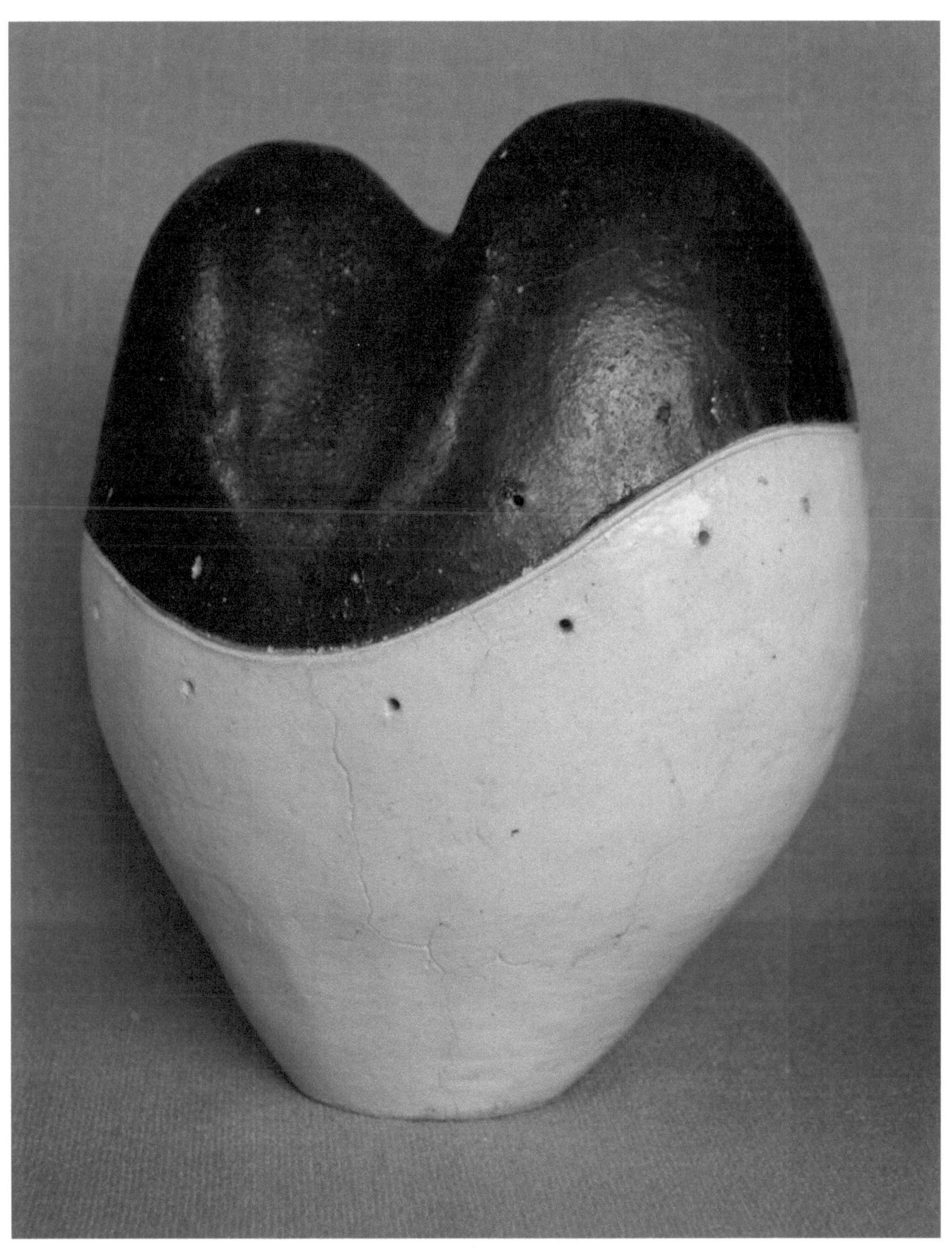

Heart transplant c 1968
stoneware
h 258 mm w 210 mm
impressed mark, inscribed 1058
Collection of the artist
Photo: Owen Barron.

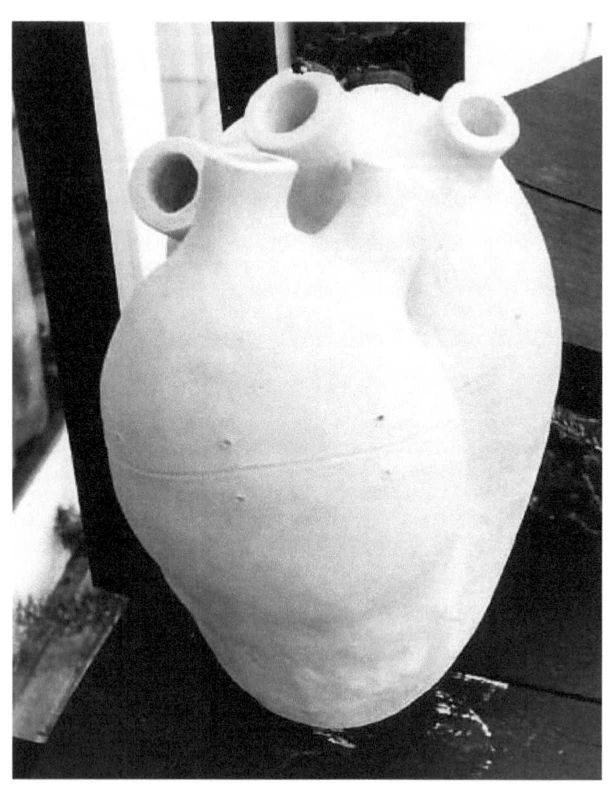

Transplant Series c 1968
Oil fired stoneware
Photo: Owen Barron.

Transplant Series c 1968
Oil fired stoneware
Rhodes 22 glaze
Photo: Owen Barron.

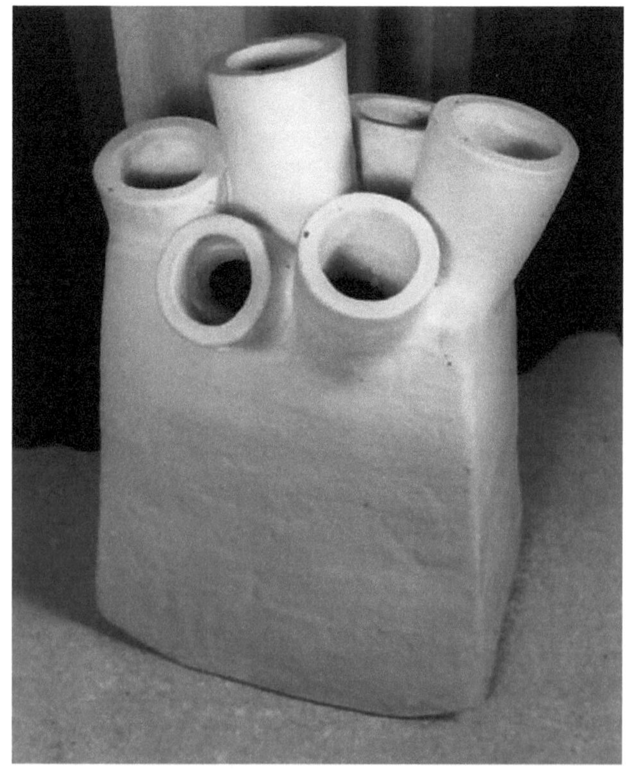

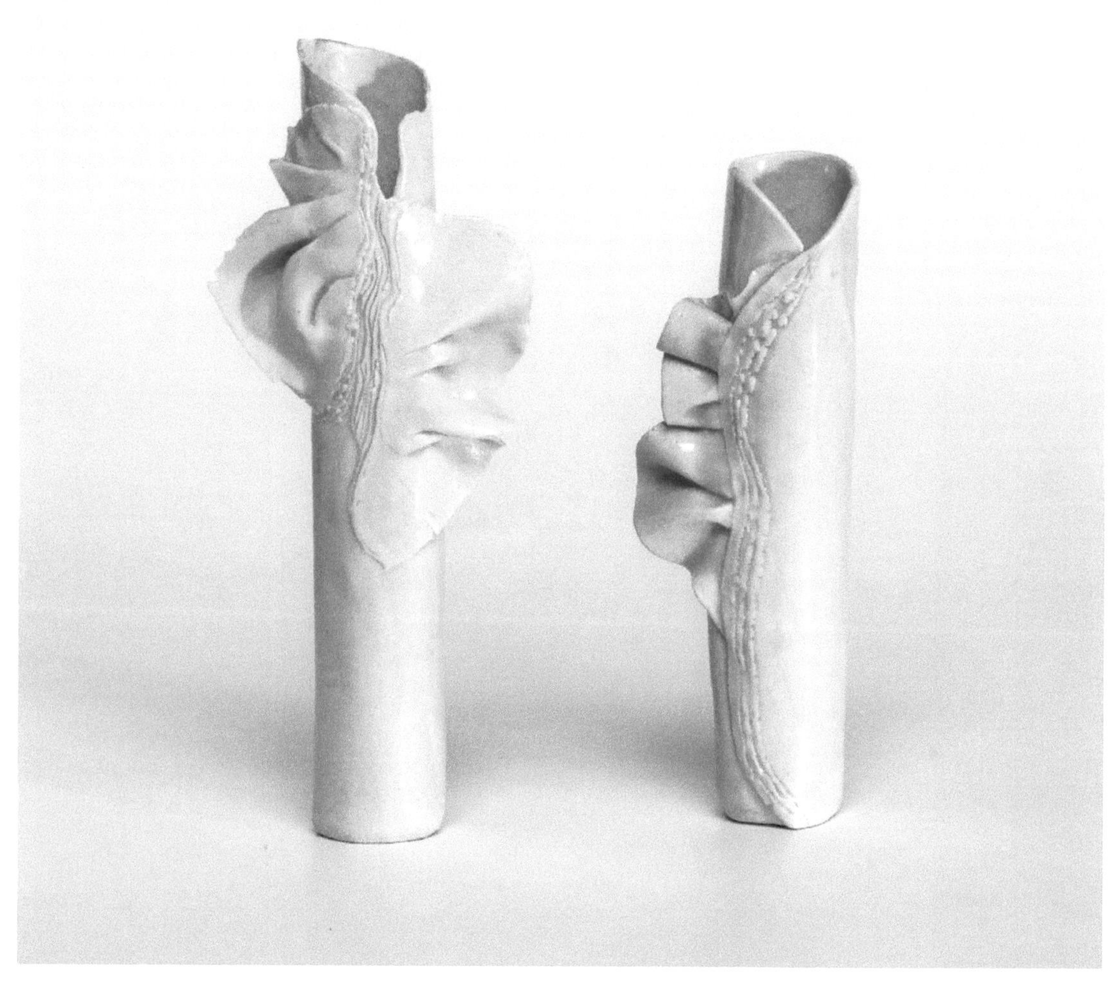

Winged Vases 1976
Porcelain - English clay
Celadon glaze (kaolin, quartz, feldspar, limestone) fired in reduced atmosphere to 1300C
left: h 200 mm w 70 mm, right: h 176 mm w 55 mm
Collection of the artist
Photo: John Collie

Reference
Illustrated, *CSA News*: The Journal of the Canterbury Society of Arts, No. 70
November/December 1976, unpaginated.
Illustrated, Peter Cape, Please Touch A Survey of Three-Dimensional Arts in New Zealand,
William Collins, 1980, p. 100.

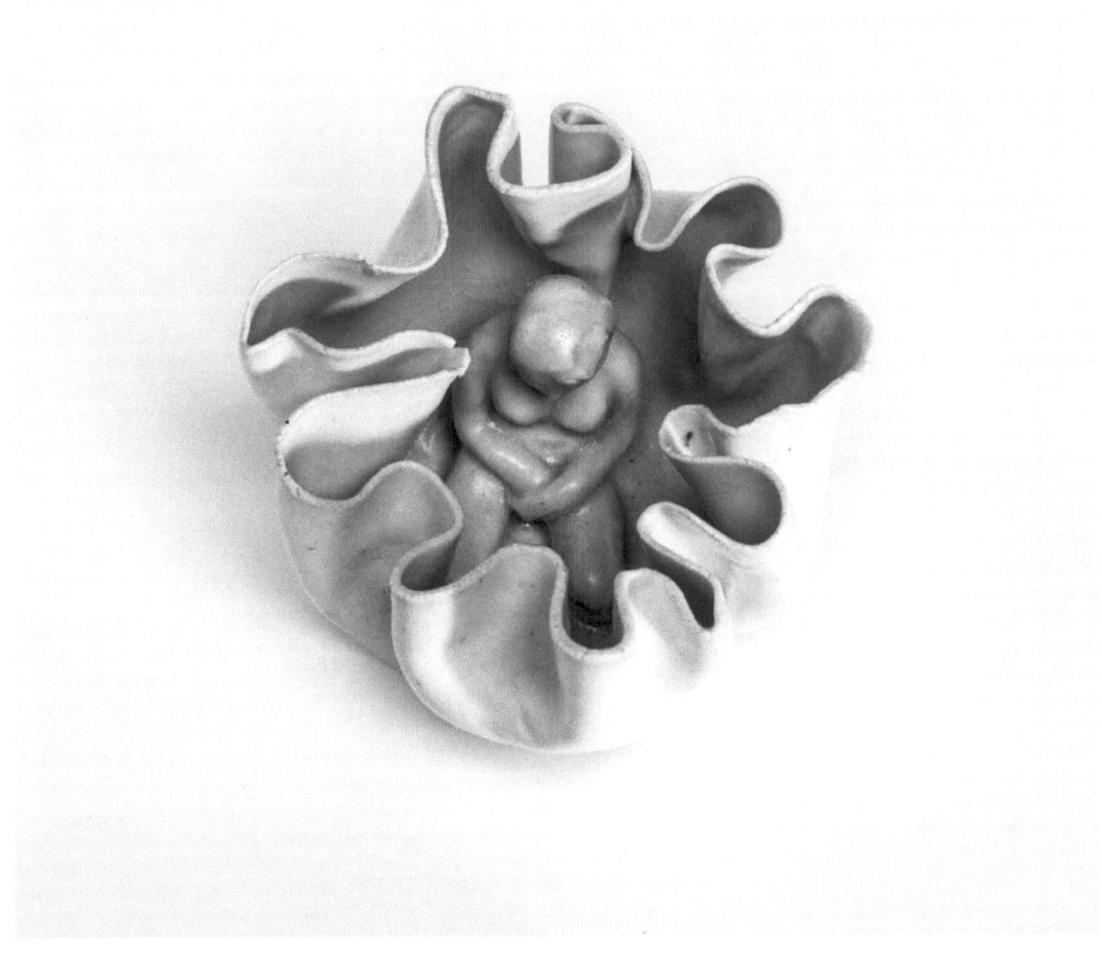

No way out 1976
Porcelain
h 75 mm   w 105 mm
incised Barron 2143 76
Collection of the artist
Photo: John Collie

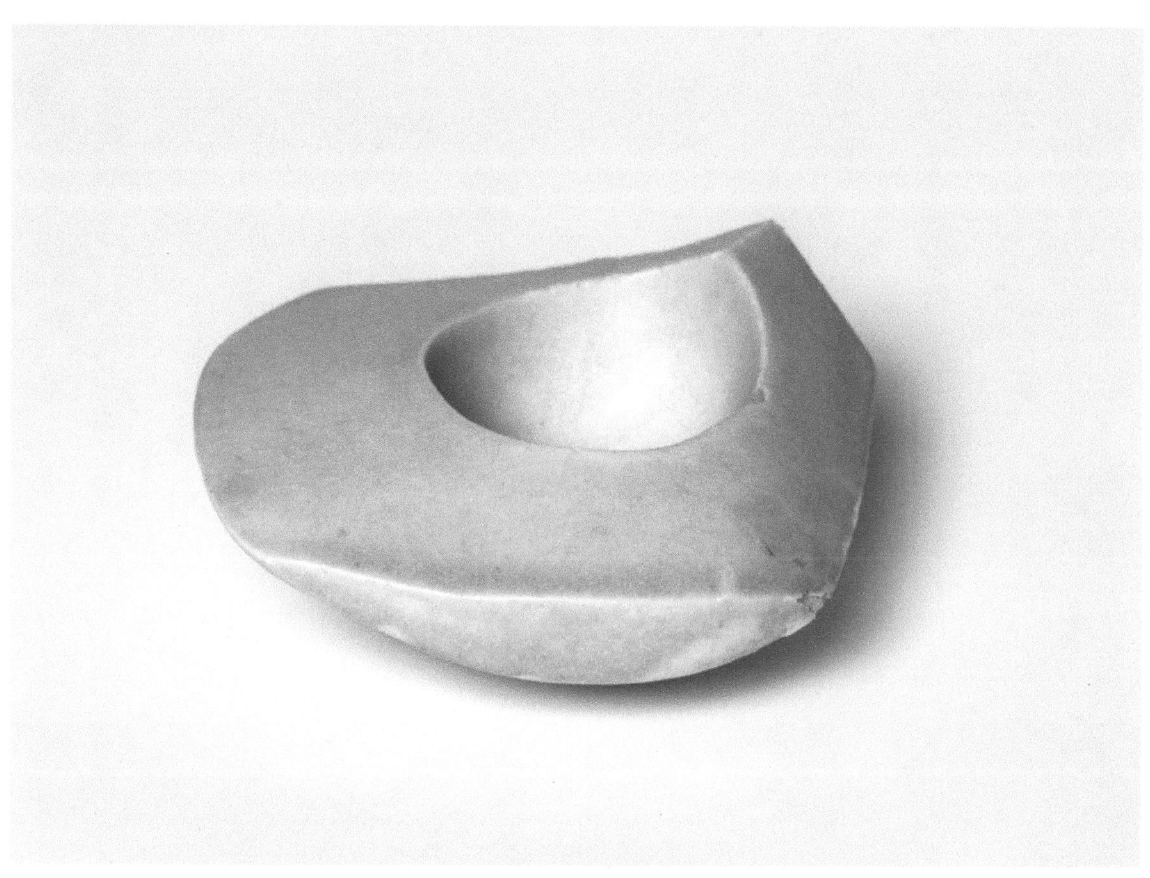

Bowl c 1976-77
porcelain
h 65 mm w 150 mm
impressed mark
Collection of Grant Banbury
Photo: John Collie

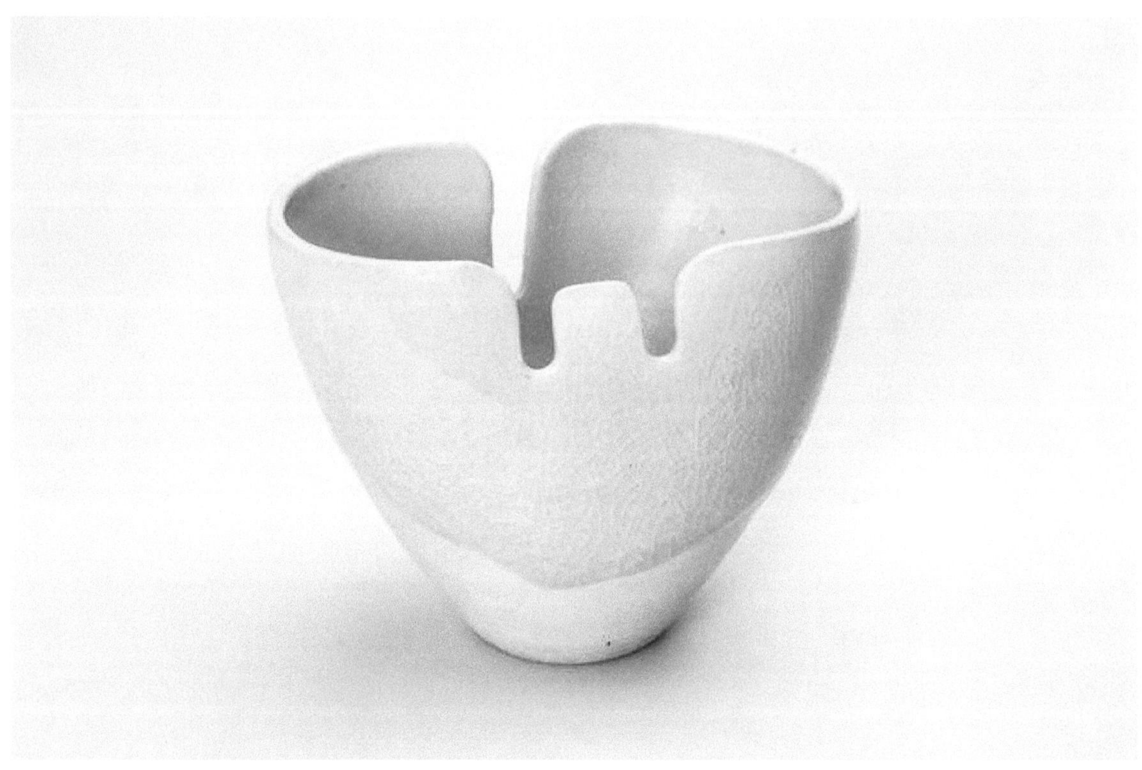

Pot 1979
Porcelain - celadon glaze
h 128 mm   w 165 mm `
impressed mark, inscribed 2224
Collection Christchurch Art Gallery Te Puna o Waiwhetu 79/354
Photo: John Collie

Note: only slip-cast ceramic Nola Barron produced.

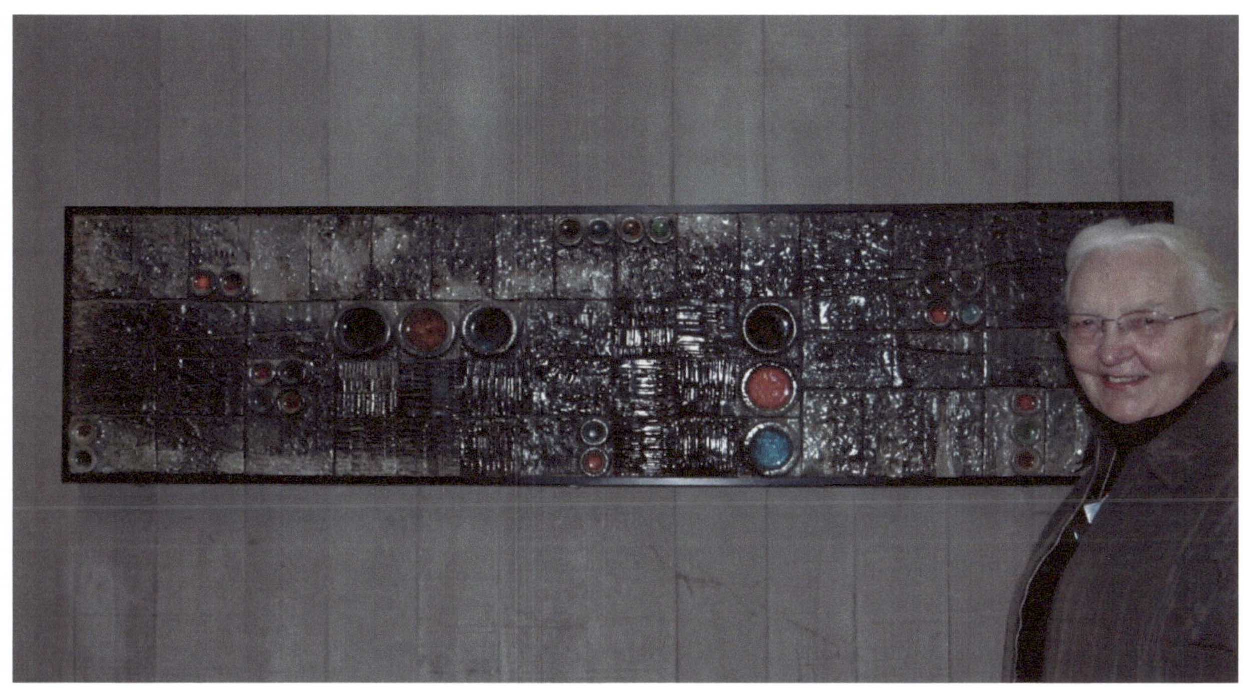

Nola with Maisie Hill Memorial Ceramic Panel 2006
1969 Commission
Ceramic, glass
440 x 1670 x 50 mm (including frame)
Collection Christchurch Girls' High School

Notes
Maisie Hill was a former student of Christchurch Girls' High School and tragically died in the Wahine disaster on 10 April 1968. Hill left a legacy to the school which became the Maisie Hill Bequest for purchasing.

Reference
Illustrated *New Zealand Potter*, Volume 11. Number 2, Spring 1969, p. 35 - two images, one showing the whole work and the other a detail.

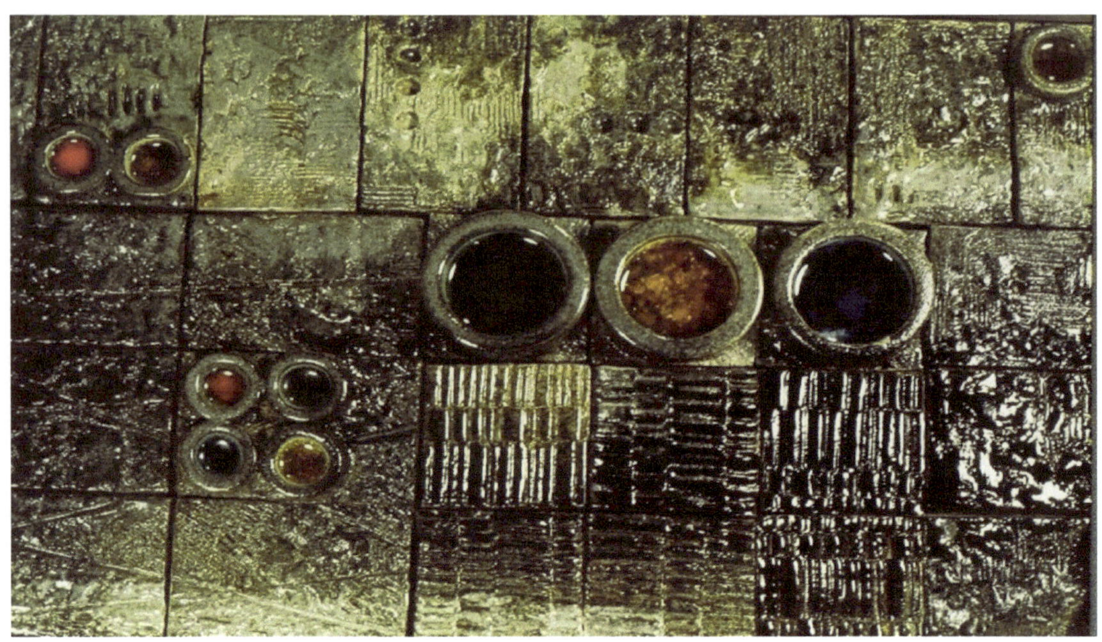

Maisie Hill Memorial Ceramic Panel 2006
Detail of tiles (see the previous image)

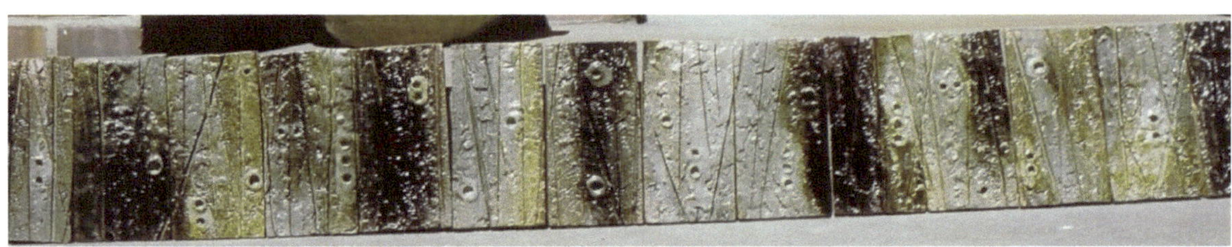

Tiles (detail) 1972
Stoneware
h 200 mm x 1200 mm (approx)
Purchased by Doris Holland and installed in the fire-surround of her Gloucester Street home,
Christchurch.
Private Collection, Christchurch
Photo: Nola Barron Archives

Reference
See Peter Bannan photograph, 'Doris Lusk at home in Christchurch: 14 February 1985' in Lisa
Beaven and Grant Banbury Landmarks: The Landscape Paintings of Doris Lusk, Robert McDougall
Art Gallery/Hazzard Press, 1996, p. 49.

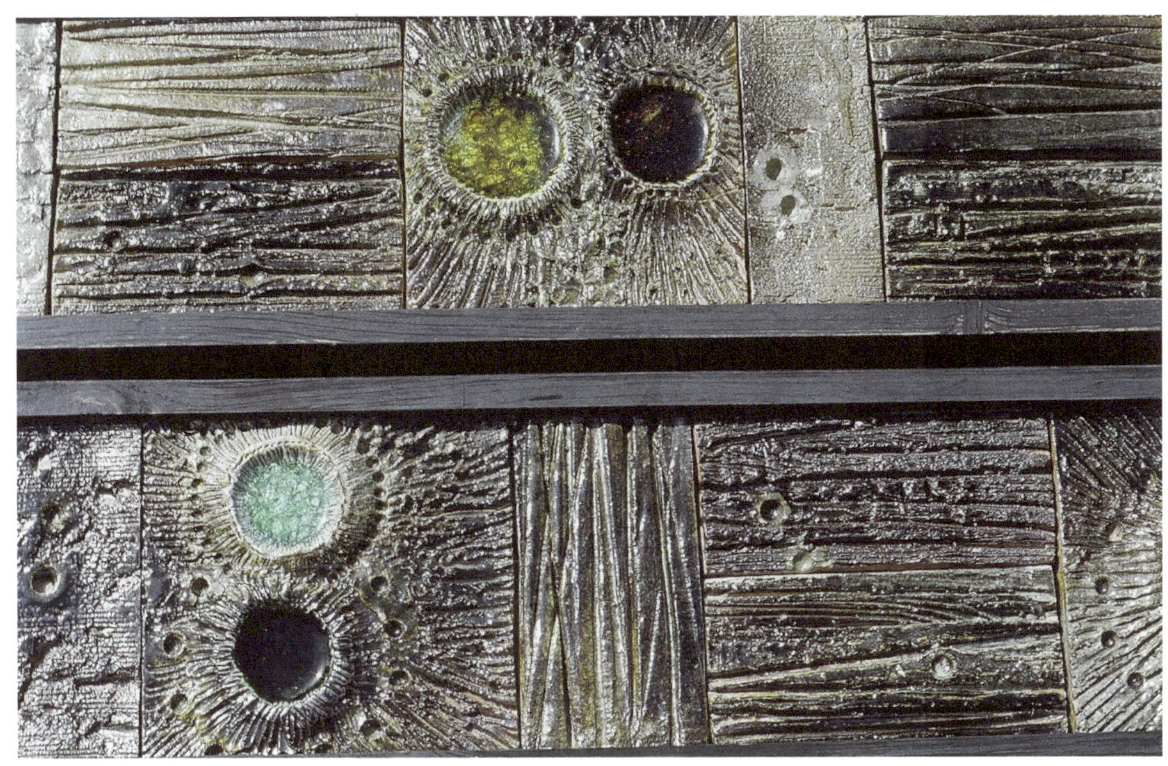

Tiles (detail) 1970s
Stoneware
(details unknown)
Photo: Nola Barron Archives

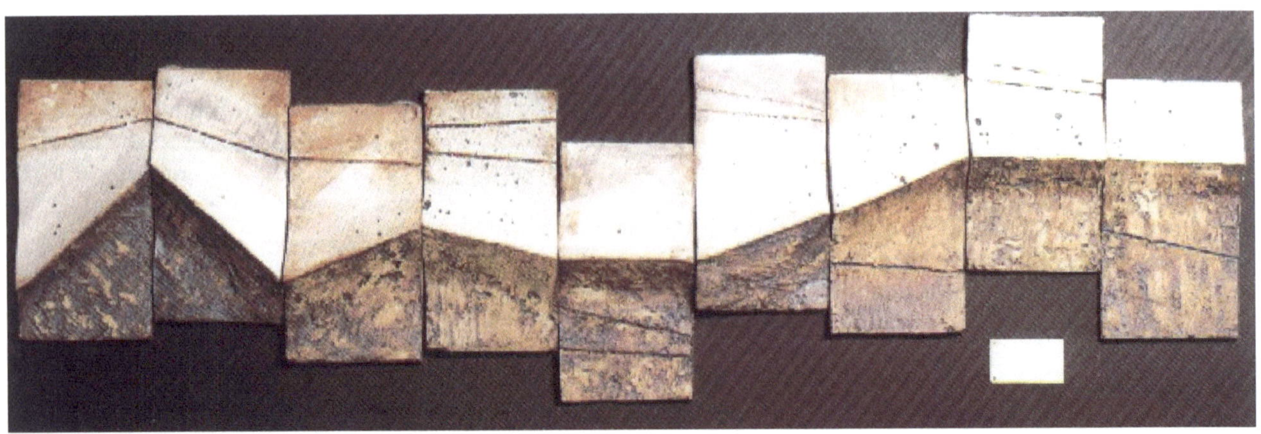

First Snow 1979
Stoneware, nine panels
1080 x 300 mm (approx size)

Exhibited
1979 Canterbury Potters Association Exhibition, cat. 24.
1979 'Crafts 1979' New Zealand Academy of Fine Arts, Wellington, cat. 110.
Purchased by Lombard Finance, Wellington
Current whereabouts unknown

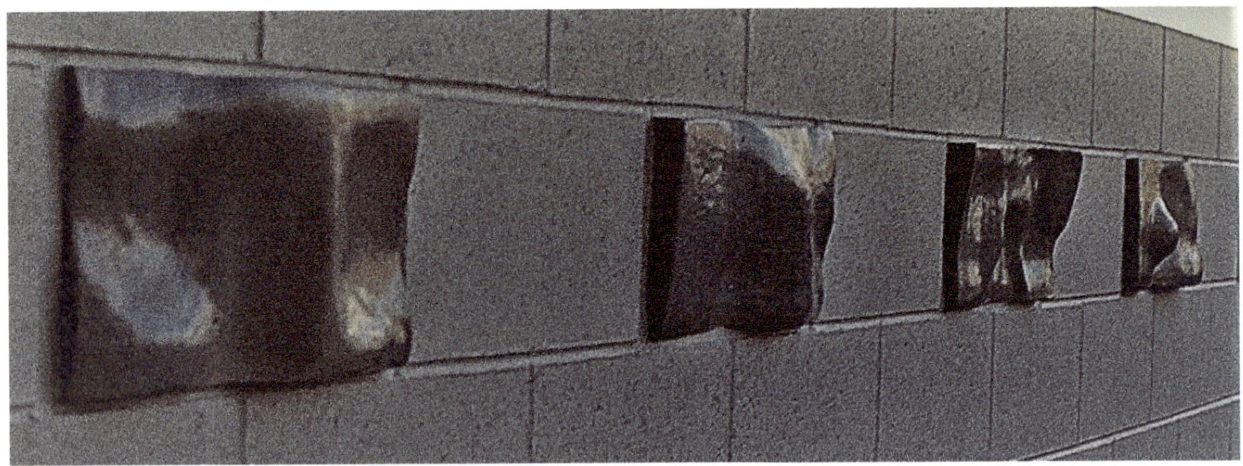

Four Ceramic tiles 1973
Exterior wall
Mt Pleasant home, Christchurch

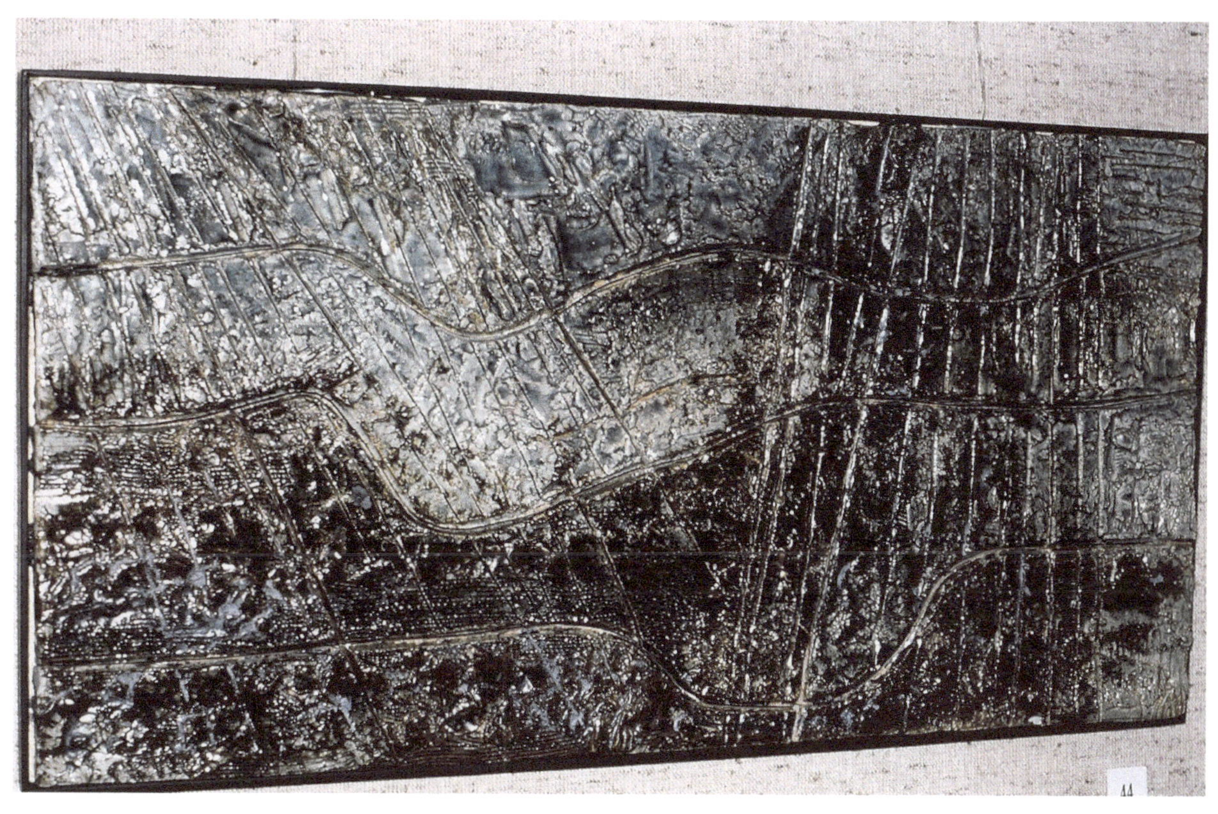

Tile panel
Stoneware
Private collection, Wanaka

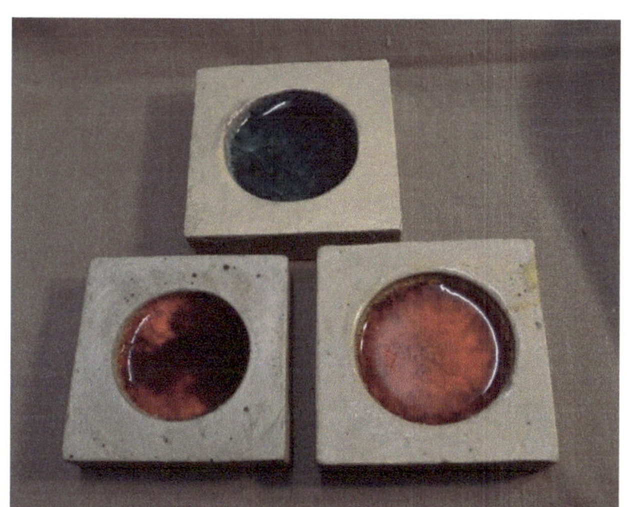

Small Ashtrays 1977
Stoneware
Molten Glass Inserts
120 mm square

SECTION TWO **SCULPTOR**

"I suppose we'll have to call her a sculptor now." I overheard this remark by Tom Taylor's to Carl Sydow[7] when they visited my home to look at some of my recent work. I realised that although I still considered myself a potter this was not strictly correct as I had not made 'pots' for some time. Over time, my pottery had developed from making domestic objects to decorative pieces with a more sculptural aspect. I was still using clay as a medium for my work but, after deciding that sculpture was the field I wished to follow, I began to experiment with other materials. At the same time, I recognised that I needed more tuition in design and the understanding of art. I applied to attend the University of Canterbury School of Fine Arts and was delighted to be accepted by Professor John Simpson, Dean of the School, as a part-time mature student. It was not my intention to sit examinations, but simply to attend lectures, do classwork, learn new techniques and become more informed. I studied design with Don Peebles and sculpture with Tom Taylor for four years part-time. I also attended life-drawing classes with Richard Lovell-Smith and printmaking with Derek Mitchell, each for one day a week for two years. Later I attended a course of printmaking at the Christchurch Polytechnic Institute of Technology under the tuition of noted printmaker Barry Cleavin.

At university, we listened to lectures and were issued with assignments. Students were encouraged to produce original work based on researching the information we required from the resources available. The role of the lecturer was to suggest an area of study, oversee the work, and challenge the students' conclusions. Having adjusted to the learning system, I enjoyed the experience and gained much valuable knowledge and confidence. Following my experience at art school, I experimented with the use of GRP (glass-reinforced plastic), commonly called fibreglass, to produce sculptural objects. These included a design for a repeatable series of fibreglass panels to decorate the front wall a new factory in Bromley, Christchurch. I also made a fibreglass sculpture for a home in Cashmere and several other fibreglass sculptures, including a garden fountain based on a diagram of neurons.

At this time, I was also working on quite large pieces in clay and experimenting with other materials. For a brief spell, I used polystyrene to create a form which was then sand-cast in aluminium alloy by a Christchurch foundry. The heat of the metal destroys the foam and the resulting cavity is filled to create a metal copy of the original model. It was not a particularly interesting technique. One large piece, Sun Disc, made by this process was bought by artist Olivia Spencer Bower and looked good in her Christchurch garden.

At art school, the method of bronze casting we used was the centuries-old lost-wax method. The artist creates a model made of wax, which is then encased in a thick plaster-of-Paris and brick-powder layer. Risers to ventilate the mould so that it does not explode, and runners to pour the molten metal in are added. The wax is burnt out in a low-firing kiln, leaving a void that is filled with melted bronze. After the cast has cooled the mould is broken off. The model can be used once only, so each piece is unique. The bronze comes out rough with bars where the risers and runners were, so there is a considerable amount of finishing and patination work required.

I tried to discover the mystery of lost-wax casting using ceramic shell moulds. A ceramic coating less than 3 mm thick is poured over the wax and high-fired to form a ceramic shell strong enough, when

---

[7] Tom Taylor (1924-1994) was a senior lecturer in sculpture at the University of Canterbury School of Fine Arts and Carl Sydow (1940-1975) was a diploma student.

supported, to take the pour of molten bronze. At that time, bronze casting using ceramic moulds was commercially sensitive and highly secret. When I attended a summer school for ceramic casting in Whanganui, I learned that the secret special ingredient was zircon flour. At this school, I made two abstract female figures and cast them in bronze using this method. On my return, I successfully cast some small bronze figures of protesting women. These pieces were based on a succession of photographs appearing in the daily newspapers at the time. While I supported the women's movement, I was disheartened at the aggression displayed by some women.

Another method of achieving a bronze casting is to make a clay model, which when dry, is taken to a foundry where a pull-apart mould is supplied. This means that the bronze does not need to be solid metal, although the wall is relatively thick. However, it does preclude undercut areas which hinder the removal of the casting from the mould. My series of bronzes called Landforms were made by this method. They required many hours of work filing, electric sanding and buffing to obtain the smoothly polished surface I sought. Some of these larger bronzes were exhibited in Christchurch and Wellington, but only one or two were sold.

The Sculptors' Group

The Sculptor's group (New Zealand Society of Sculptors and Painters) was formed in August 1970. Tom Taylor was the first president and the foundation members were Christine Hellyar, Ria Bancroft, Colleen Newton, Carl Sydow, Allan Strathern, John Turner, John Doudney, Lawrence Karasek, Neil Dawson, Jack Nuttall, David Jackson, Michael Trumic, Nola Barron, and Tony Fomison. An exhibition of this group's work travelled throughout the country in 1971 and another was presented by the CSA Gallery in 1972. The society has disbanded, although individual members continue to work and examples of their work are familiar to the present generation. The work of the painter members appears in public art-gallery collections throughout the country. Neil Dawson's large sculptures in aluminium and stainless steel are well known both here and overseas. Christchurch people will recognise his works, including Chalice in Cathedral Square and Fanfare situated beside the motorway on the northern approach to Christchurch. Alan Strathern's large sculptural group entitled Trawlermen is a prominent feature on the Napier foreshore. A work made by Ria Bancroft[8] in co-operation with Pat Mulcahy, a wood sculptor, was displayed in the Cathedral of the Blessed Sacrament in Barbadoes Street, Christchurch, until the time of the earthquake. Michael Trumic established a successful pottery in Loburn. He also set up the Otago Polytechnic's ceramics department in the 1970s and later received an honorary degree, a Diploma of Fine Arts (with Honours) from the Polytechnic. My career as a sculptor was interrupted when I became director of the CSA Gallery in 1977, and my time and energy were given over to the new position.

Summary

Section Two deals with my decision to concentrate on sculpture and experiments with a variety of materials including GRP, aluminium alloy, and bronze. It also covers the time I spent as a part-time student at the University of Canterbury School of Fine Arts.

---

[8] See Peb Simmons, **No Ordinary Woman: Ria Bancroft,** David Bateman, 1997.

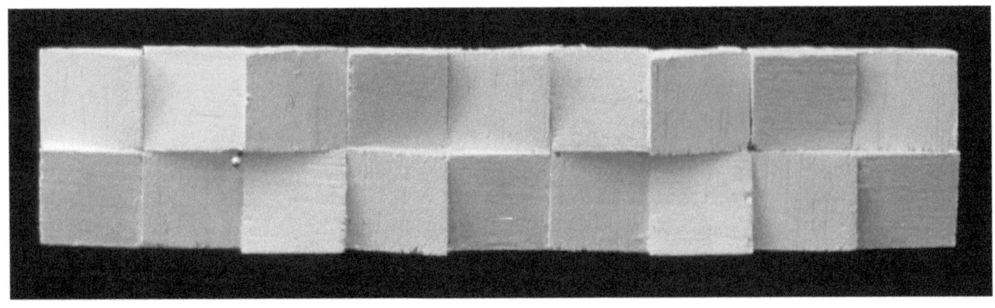

Maquette for Futuro Mural 1975
Photo: Nola Barron Archives

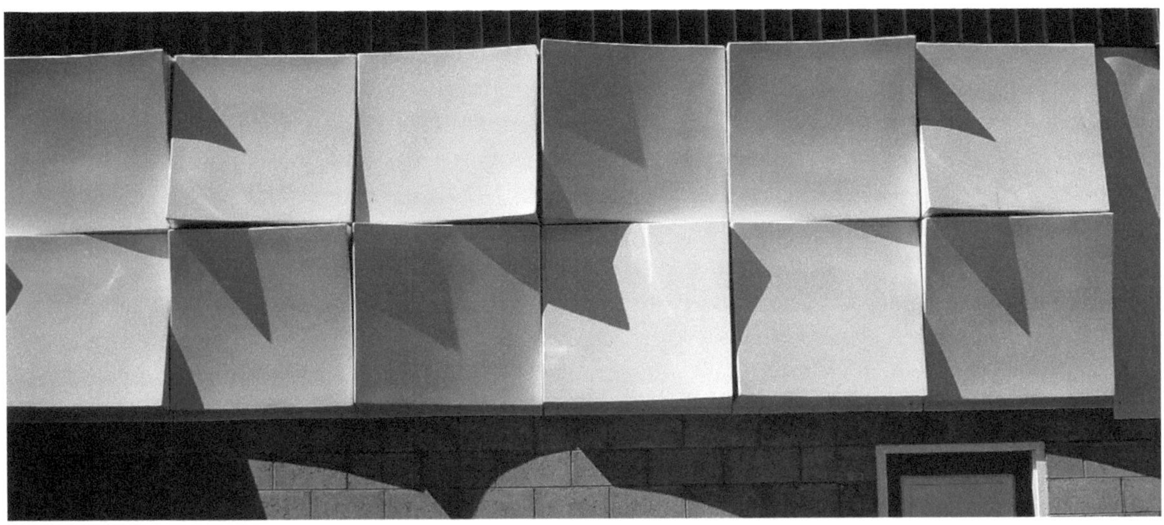

Futuro Mural c 1975
Fibreglass painted white
Image: sculpture installed on Futuro building, Bromley, Christchurch
Photo: Nola Barron Archives.

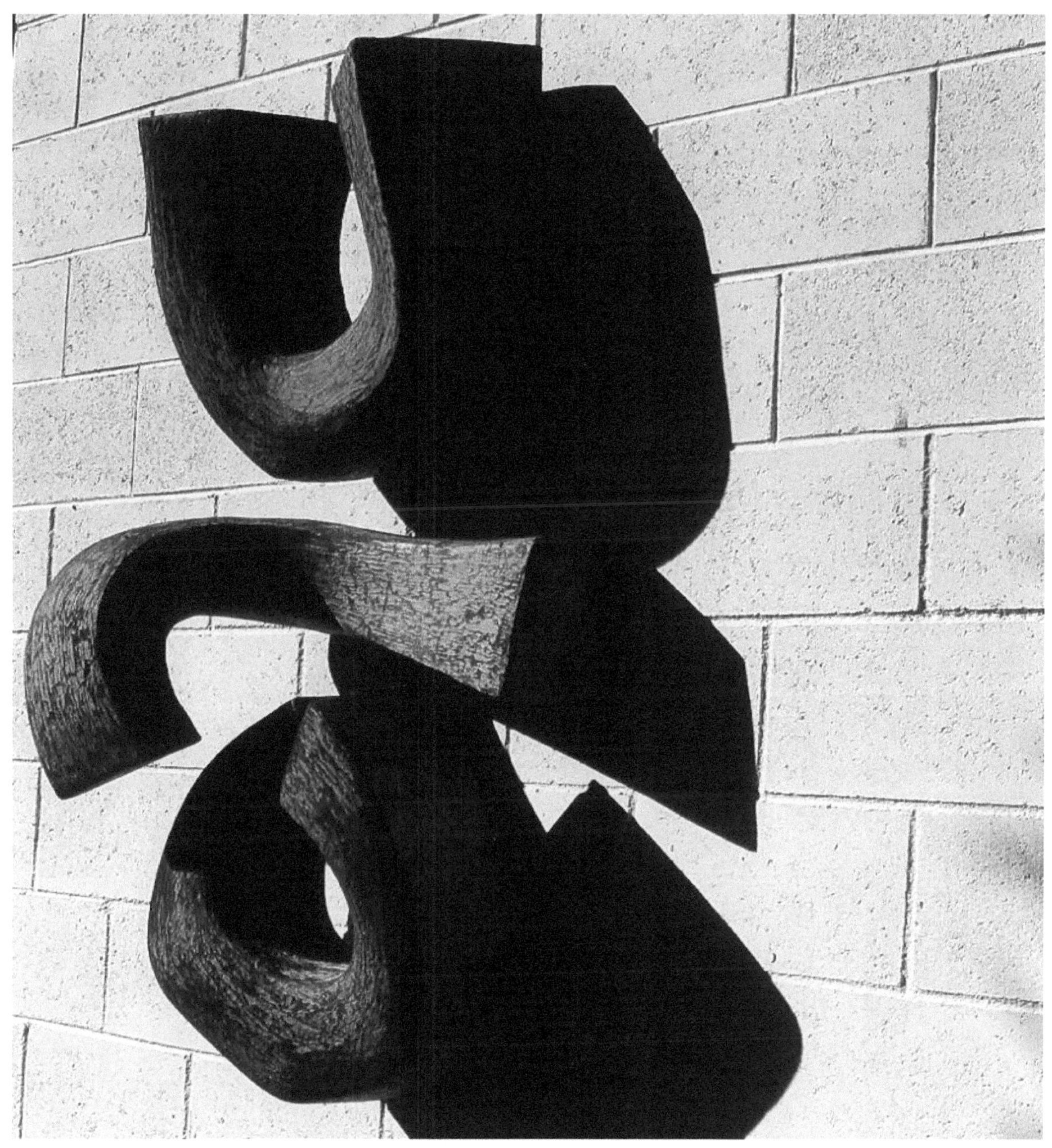

Sculpture 1968
fibreglass
h 1030 mm
Private collection, Christchurch
Image: work installed on an exterior wall, private house, Cashmere, Christchurch
Photo: Nola Barron.

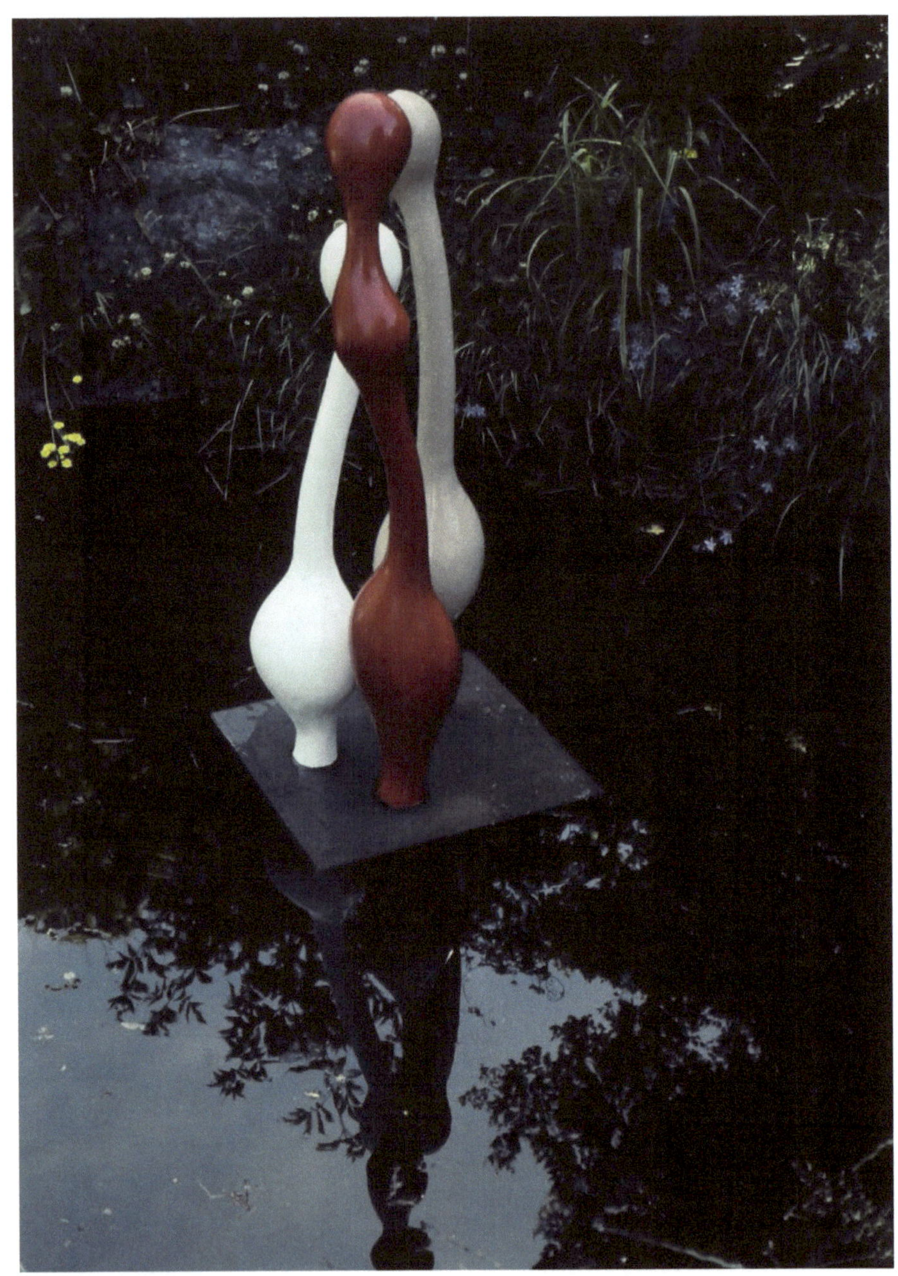

Neurons 1970
fibreglass fountain
h 600 mm
Photo: Nola Barron Archives.

Exhibited
1972 NZSSP exhibition, CSA Gallery, Christchurch 1970, cat. 1.
Notes: Image shows Neurons installed in the artist's garden, Heaton Street, Christchurch

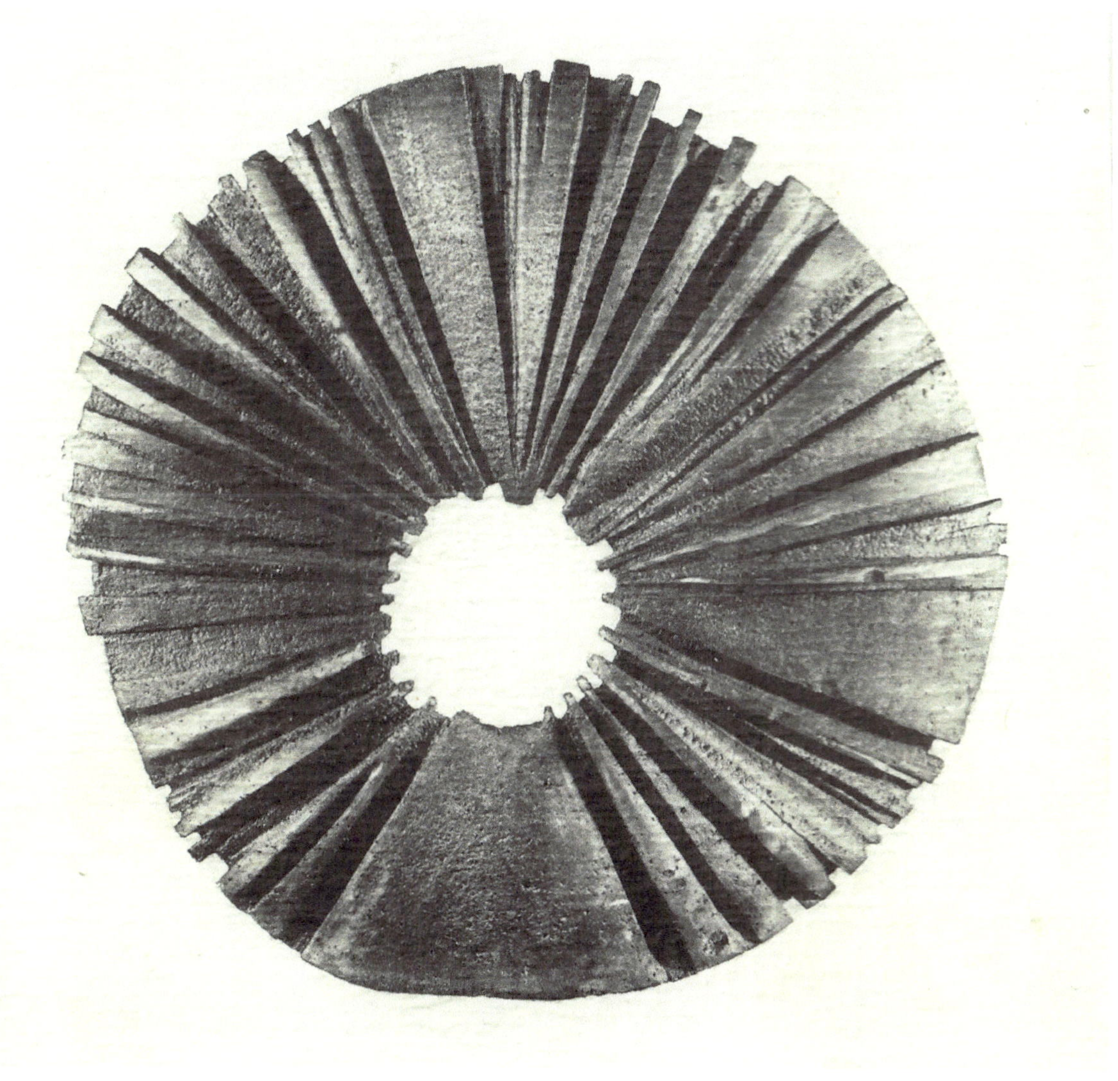

Sun disc July 1972
Cast aluminium polished with paint stain and coated with polyurethane (cast by A Farrar Ltd)
Current whereabouts unknown
Note: image reproduced from the cover of the exhibition catalogue

Exhibited
1973 Canterbury Society of Arts 93rd Autumn Exhibition (cover illustration on catalogue)

Collection
Formally in the collection of Olivia Spencer Bower, Christchurch. Displayed as garden feature
Note: Olivia Spencer Bower's art collection was sold in 1985 to support an annual award for artists

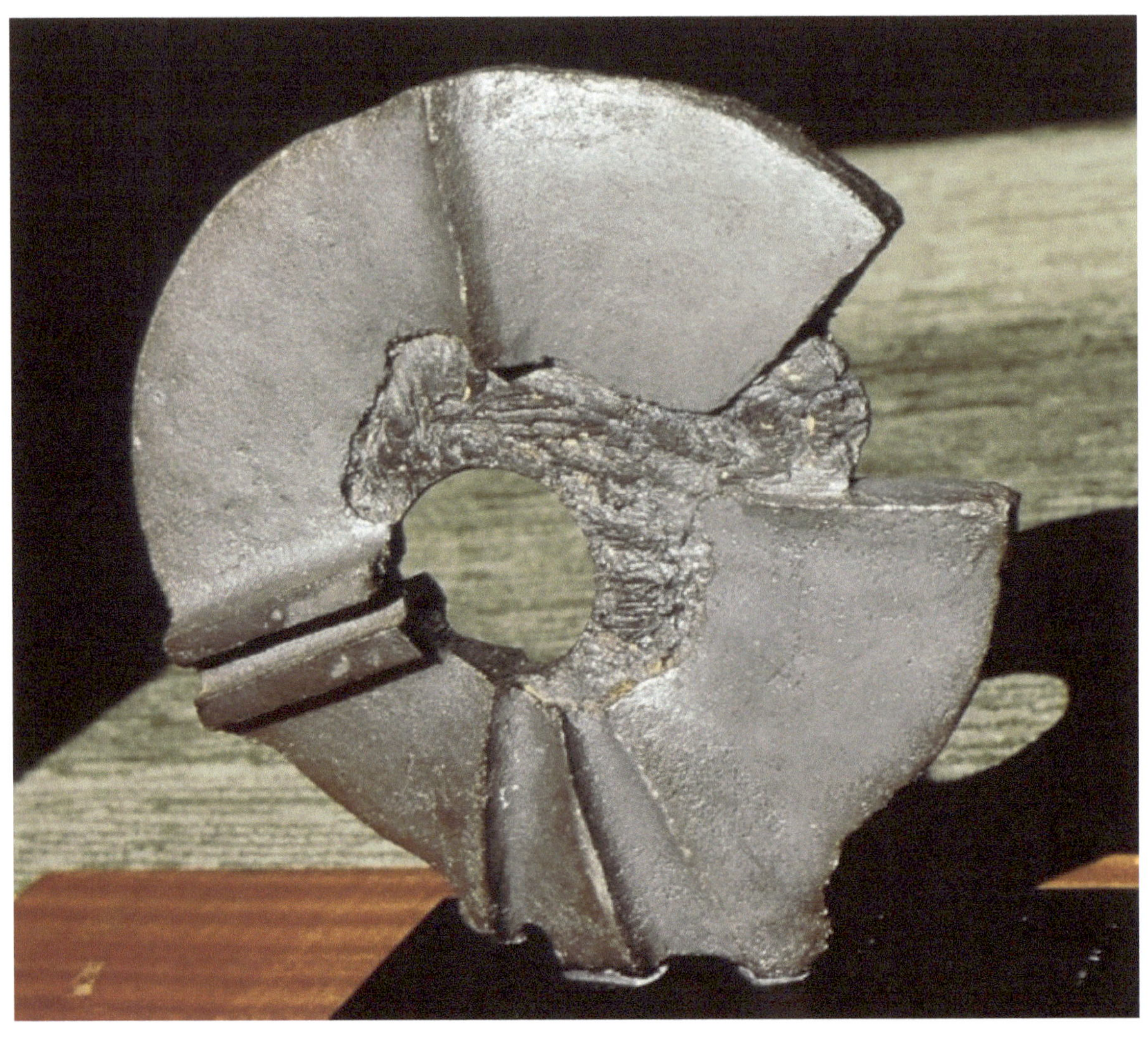

Cast aluminium disk c 1973
400 mm x 250 mm
Current whereabouts unknown
Photo: Nola Barron Archives

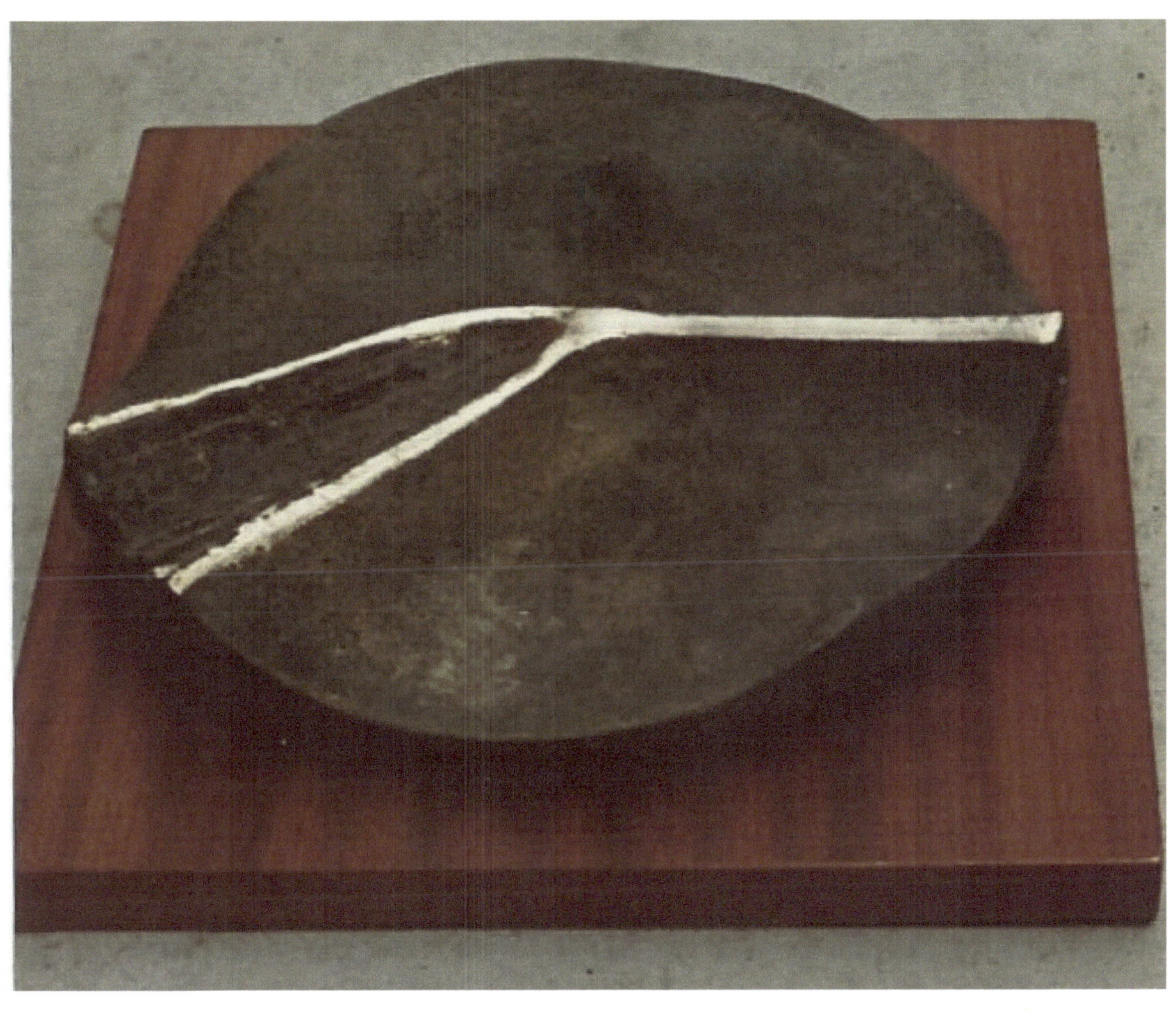

Land Disc with lightning Dec 1974
Exhibited at CSA 1974 and Waimate 1978
Private collection Timaru

Coastal Series

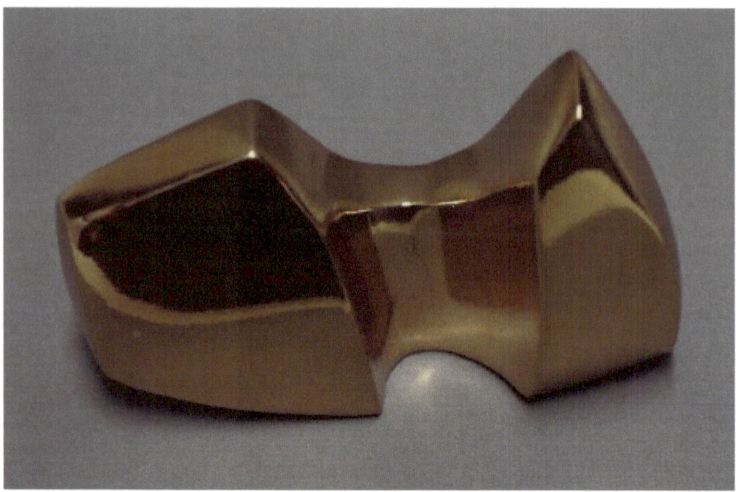

Big Bay - Marlborough coast 1974
bronze
Collection of the artist
Photo: Owen Barron

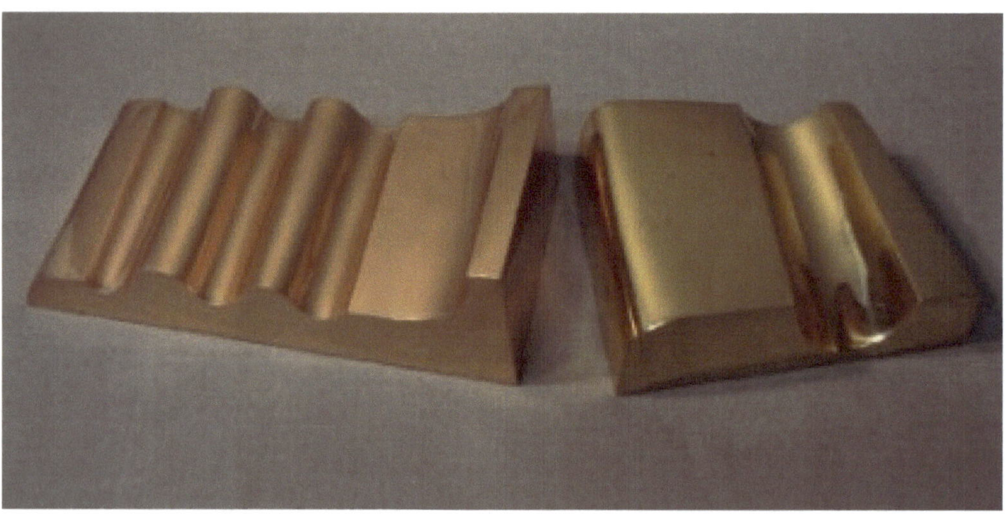

North Canterbury - Kaikoura coastline (diptych)
bronze
Left: 72 x 280 x 163 mm Right: 57 x 195 x 163 mm
Collection of the artist
Photo: Owen Barron

Reference: Illustrated Peter Cape, Please touch, A survey of three-dimensional arts in New Zealand,
Collins, 1980, p. 37.

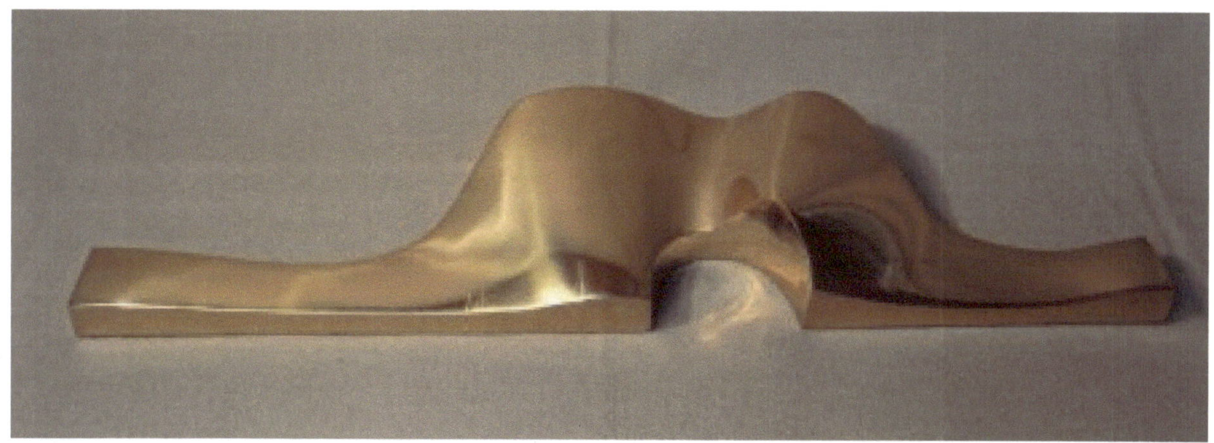

Landform - Marlborough
bronze
64 x 678 x 187 mm
Collection of the artist
Photo: Owen Barron

Reference
Illustrated Peter Cape, Please Touch A survey of three-dimensional arts in New Zealand, Collins, 1980, p. 37.

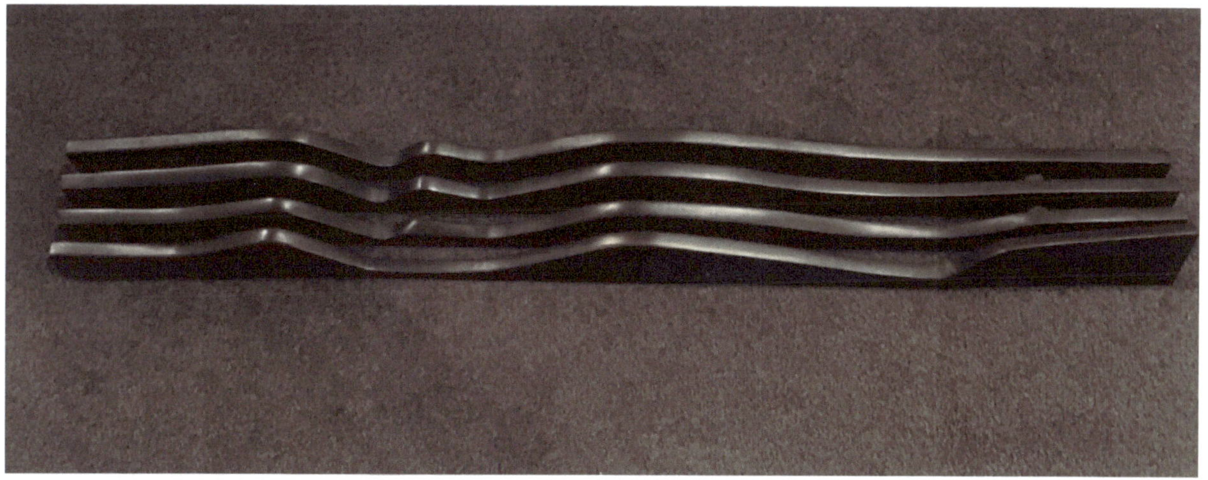

Foothills Waipara
bronze
patinated with polished edges
Collection Andrew & Carol Barron
Photo: Owen Barron

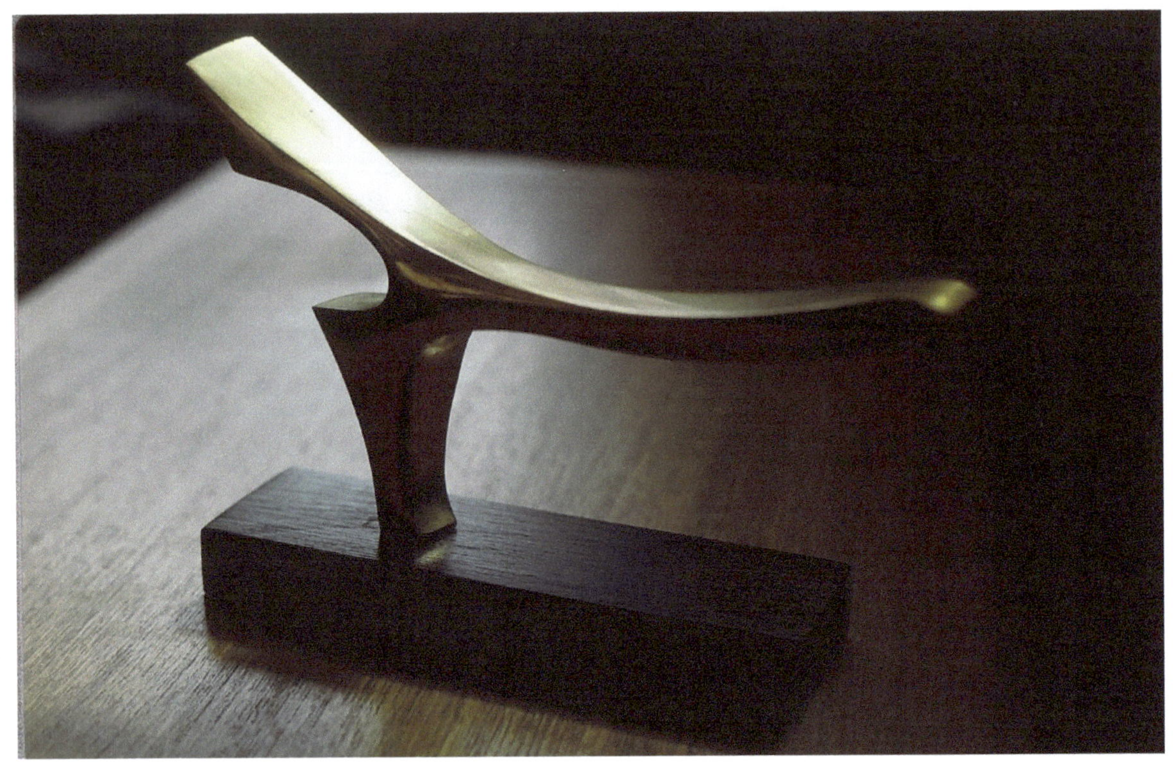

Untitled [Form] c 1970
bronze, wood stand
h 150 x w 240 mm d 45 mm
University of Canterbury Art Collection UC-CCE-055
Photo: Nola Barron archives

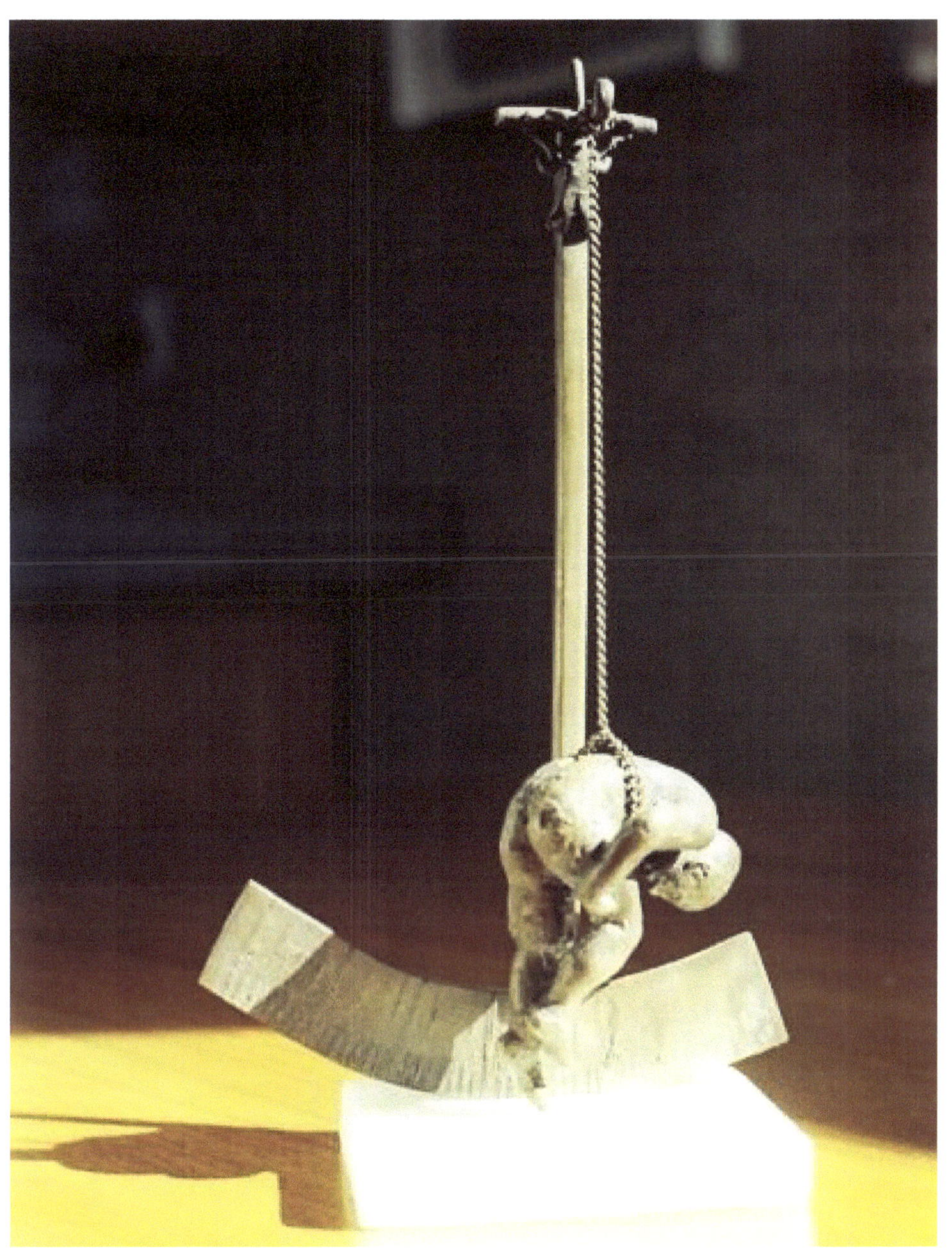

Eight-to-Five Man 1977
cast bronze
h 150 mm
Photo: Nola Barron Archives

Exhibition
The Group Show, 1977, CSA Gallery, cat. 85.
Private collection

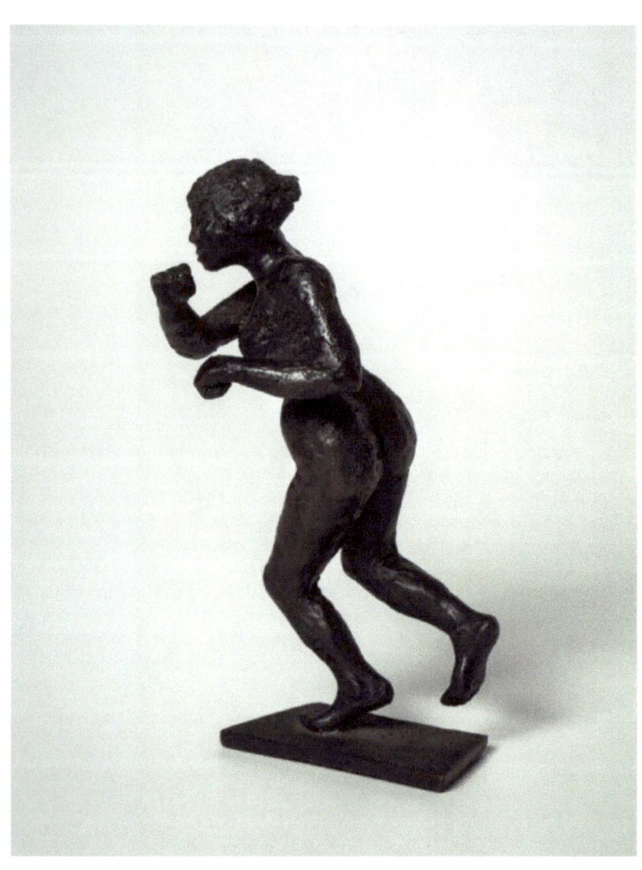

Protesting woman
cast bronze, patinated
185 x 102 x 175 mm
Collection of the artist
Photo: John Collie

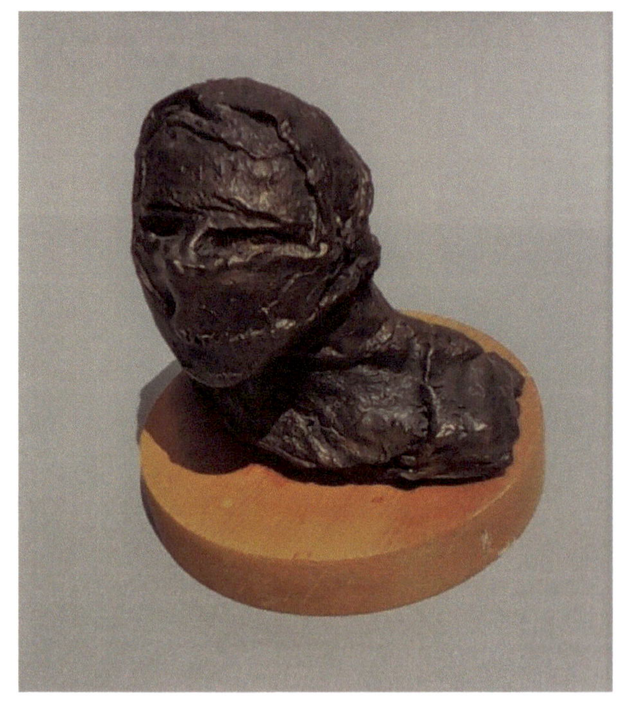

Masked woman c 1973
cast bronze, patinated
h 80 mm x w 85 mm (including base)
Collection of the artist
Photo: Owen Barron

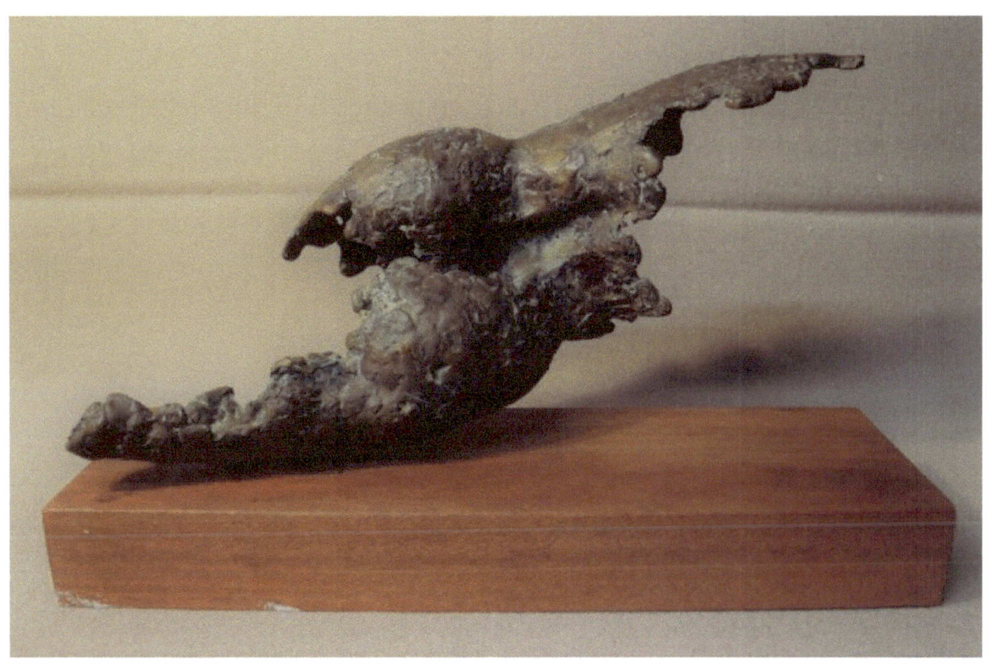

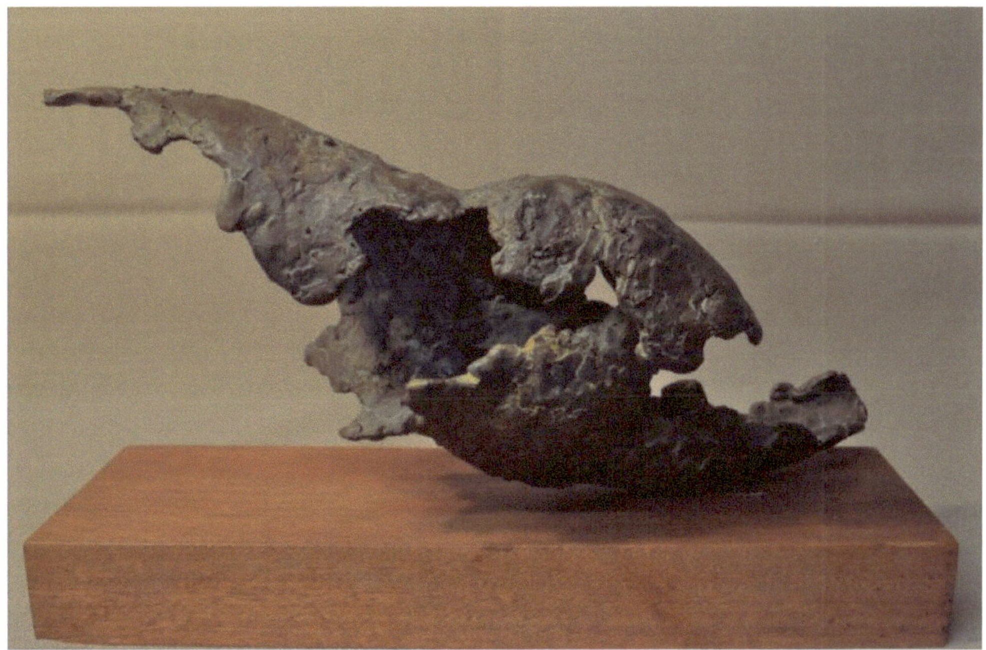

Reclining woman c 1973
cast bronze, wood base
249 x 397 x 180 mm (including base)

A brief history of the CSA

The Canterbury Society of Arts was established in 1880 and continued until 1996 when the name, focus and legal status transferred to the Canterbury Society of Arts Charitable Trust.[9]

The gallery became the Centre of Contemporary Art (CoCA) and continues to exhibit art. The Society's stated aim was 'to promote the study, practice and cultivation of the fine arts ... and to encourage the production of works of art by periodical exhibitions'. I was director of the CSA Gallery from 1977 to 1986.

The society had two classes of membership:

> a. Working members: practising artists, both professional and amateur, and
> b. Ordinary members: people interested in art.

Following a severe earthquake in 1886, the Society built an art gallery on the corner of Armagh and Durham streets. This gallery served the Society well for many years. Its main purpose was to show work by working members, and exhibitions were held four times a year. Occasionally, the gallery exhibited work by individual artists or groups of professional artists. The Society also accumulated a large collection of works by local and international artists. Many works from this collection were loaned or gifted to the Robert McDougall Art Gallery when it opened in 1932 in the Botanic Gardens. By 1965 the population of the city had increased more than twentyfold and the McDougall, the only public art gallery in Christchurch, had reached its maximum potential. There was also pressure from the Department of Justice, which wished to enlarge its facilities and requested the Society vacate the Durham Street land. These facts, together with the realisation by CSA council that to fulfil its aims the Society should expand its facilities, led to the decision to replace the old gallery.

66 Gloucester Street

A new purpose-built gallery, designed by Minson, Henning-Hansen and Dines, was built at 66 Gloucester Street. At the time of building, it included three floors with six exhibition spaces varying from 56 square metres to 256 square metres. Amenities included goods-lift access to the first floor, a workshop, storage space for the Society's collection, a kitchen, office and restrooms (a lift was installed later). By providing such a large building the CSA council confirmed its belief that the best way to promote the Society's aims was to offer the best facilities for artists to display and sell their work. This ambitious project demonstrated confidence and foresight by the Society at that time.

The CSA Gallery had two objectives. One was to provide a venue for the working members and other artists and craftspeople to display their work and make it available for sale. The second imperative was to provide a venue where the people of Christchurch could experience art and purchase items. The gallery was open every day from 10 am to 4 pm as well as 7 pm to 9 pm on preview evenings with no entry fee. It was a wonderful space where artists could display their work to the best effect. It also provided a facility for selling work and looked after its presentation and delivery to the customer, as well as all the financial aspects.

---

[9] For a complete history of the CSA see Dr Warren Feeney, *The Radical, the Reactionary and the Canterbury Society of Arts 1880-1996,* Canterbury University Press, 2011.

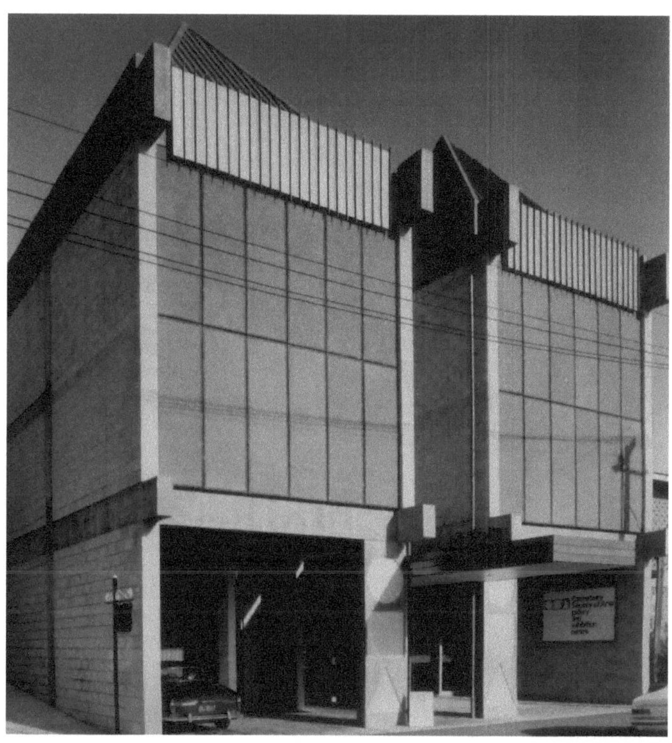

The new gallery was opened by the Governor-General Sir Arthur Porritt on March 8, 1968. Guests included George Manning, Mayor of Christchurch, the Hon A. E. Kinsella, Minister of Education, and Norman Kirk, Leader of the Opposition. The CSA held a ballot among its members for admission to the opening. The opening coincided with a Pan Pacific Arts Festival and the gallery mounted several important shows to mark the occasion.

These included a touring exhibition of French sculpture and works on loan from the National Gallery of Australia, with paintings by noted Australian painter Sidney Nolan in the ground-floor gallery.

The first custodian of the new gallery was Russell (Rusty) Laidlaw who acted in this capacity for the first eight years. Rusty had been secretary/manager of the previous Durham Street gallery. However, it became evident that to sustain financial viability the

The CSA gallery at 66 Gloucester Street, Christchurch

gallery must be open continually, not just for sporadic exhibitions. As Rusty had no wish to be permanently employed, he retired. He was my mentor and model. His charm and dedication had built up the membership and popularity of the CSA especially after the move from Durham Street to Gloucester Street. The Society then appointed Annella MacDougall as director and she became the gallery's first fully paid employee. However, Annella decided to resign after about 14 months and the CSA council was faced with the task of finding a replacement.

My time as director

The circumstances of my appointment are best described by reference to the president's annual report to members presented at the AGM on November 29, 1977. CSA President Sir Miles Warren made the following comments:

'Last year I reported the resignation of our first full-time director, Miss MacDougall. None of the applicants for a replacement seemed to fit the bill. At the last council meeting, it dawned on a number of us that we had the perfect director right in our midst: Mrs Nola Barron. As a councillor for a number of years she knew the ins and outs of the Society, we knew that she was a good organiser and, above all, she was an artist of the highest repute. I was delighted to report earlier in the year that Nola has been coaxed, bullied, and cajoled into the job. It was the best decision the council has made for years. Nola Barron had to take over during the tricky period just before Christmas. There was little time to make the transfer from Miss MacDougall and looming in the New Year was all the organisation required for the Society's Fine Crafts exhibition. Perhaps there was poetic justice in this. This special exhibition was Nola's brainchild. She had promoted the idea, selected and invited the artists, and most importantly, coaxed them into producing their best work.' – F.M. Warren.

In a statement to the local newspaper shortly after my appointment, I outlined some of my aims and objectives:

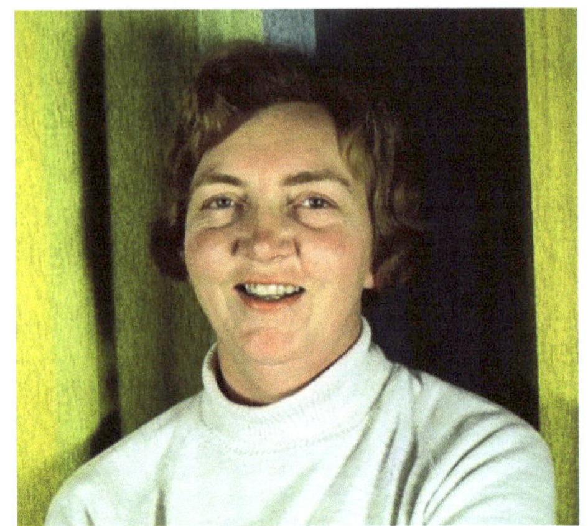

Nola Barron (1977)
Photo: Christchurch Press

'THE NEW FACE behind the director's desk at the Canterbury Society of Arts Gallery is a familiar one. Nola Barron, who has just taken over as director, is a well-known Christchurch potter and sculptor and a member of the society council. She succeeds Annella MacDougall, who left to open her own craft shop. A member of the Group, Nola Barron has also been on the executive of the New Zealand Society of Potters and is a member of the World Craft Council. She wants to make the gallery a livelier place and to attract exhibitions of the finest work available in New Zealand, plus some overseas from time to time. "I want it to be a place where the best New Zealand artists are happy to have their work seen," she said.' Garry Arthur, "Reporter's Diary", **The Press**, January 12, 1977.

My 10-year stewardship of the gallery coincided with an upsurge of interest in the arts in Christchurch. Membership of the Society more than doubled and exhibition openings attracted large numbers of excited viewers, many of whom were serious buyers. On a personal note, the new position as the director of a large art gallery brought about a complete change in my lifestyle. From being an independent and self-employed working artist, whose only responsibility was to her family, I became answerable to hundreds of people, comprising several diverse groups each with its own, often conflicting, agenda. At times I felt like a tightrope walker or juggler. It required balance between several conflicting initiatives: to present innovative and interesting exhibitions, to exhibit the work of the best artists, to endorse and show new talent, and to offer the best available work in various media. Added to this was the requirement to satisfy the needs of working members and maintain the interest of the public in order to gain their support in appreciating and buying artwork. It also illustrated a change of emphasis. In order for the gallery to be financially viable, while still achieving its remit of fostering the arts, it was necessary to take advantage of the large exhibition areas available by becoming more professional.

Financial considerations

As a charitable, not-for-profit enterprise, the gallery was not required to return a dividend to shareholders. It also enjoyed the considerable advantage of being exempt from Christchurch City Council Rates. However, it was also a business and as such, in order to remain viable, it was necessary that its income was sufficient to cover expenses. Because the gallery was open to the public for long periods with no entry fee, overhead costs – lighting, heating, cleaning, maintenance, depreciation and staff salaries – were substantial, although some savings were made by the voluntary work of Society members. Income was derived from various sources. Commercial sponsorship was rare at that time, but some support was received from Canterbury Savings Bank. Also, throughout its history, the CSA had benefited from some generous bequests which were invested. Interest from these investments was useful.

Requests for financial assistance made to agencies purporting to 'support the arts' fell on deaf ears. Many appeared to believe that as we had a large membership, we were financially secure. In fact, members' subscriptions comprised only a small proportion of the gallery's income. Some funds came from hiring the gallery's collection to commercial premises, but the main source of revenue was the gallery itself. The bulk of income came from the rent of exhibition space and the commission on sales, which was one of the reasons that up to 90 exhibitions were held each year. The late 1970s were not easy times for the gallery, but the Society continued to build up satisfactory reserves of money and artworks in its permanent collection.

At this time, the Canterbury Society of Arts had the largest membership of any Arts society in Australasia. The gallery facilities were unequalled by any art society in New Zealand. It existed without funding from local or central government. International visitors were amazed that we could offer such fine exhibition areas to such diverse arts for so little without public funding. Increased interest in art was confirmed by the increase of membership of the CSA. From 1200 members in 1966 membership had more than doubled by 1988. Income from subscriptions increased from $6500 to $36,000 but income from exhibitions was almost $100,000 and this subsidised non-revenue-producing shows.[10]

Government intervention

The 1984 Labour Government removed trade barriers and import licensing. This removed the protection previously enjoyed by New Zealand craftspeople and also impacted on sales of locally produced craft selling at the CSA Between 1979 and 1987 the CSA's annual sales from craft exhibitions averaged over $10,000, but this figure reduced considerably in later years.

Some observations

In his comprehensive history of the CSA,[11] Warren Feeney's subtitle for "Chapter Seven (1960-1970)" is "A very swinging place", and in "Chapter Eight (1976-1987)", which coincides with my tenure, he refers to the gallery as having "A curious vitality". The gallery continued as a lively venue, and I believe that the "vitality" he refers to was largely due to the efforts of a small team working hard to support the artists. The aim was to preserve the heritage of the past and to leave it a better institution for the future.

Exhibition procedure

The Society's aim was to use the gallery to introduce the citizens of Christchurch to a wide range of artistic experience and the staff endorsed this policy enthusiastically. Arrangements were flexible and varied according to the wishes of the exhibitors. Some groups preferred to rent gallery space and mount their own shows, but the usual procedure for most exhibitions was as outlined below.

Exhibitions usually ran for two weeks and several different shows were held concurrently in most of the gallery's six spaces. Every exhibition was formally opened with a preview, which was also the opportunity to purchase work. Previews were usually held on alternate Tuesday evenings at 7 pm and shows remained open until the following Sunday week.

---

[10] Many exhibitions produced little income; these included student work and performance art and were included in the calendar for artistic considerations.
[11] Dr Warren Feeney, *The Radical, the Reactionary and the Canterbury Society of Arts 1880-1996,* Canterbury University Press, 2011.

Purchased work was available for collection at the conclusion of the show and unsold items stored prior to return to the artist. The next Tuesday saw the installation of a new exhibition ready for opening that evening.

Invitations to previews were sent to all Society members and guests of the exhibitor. Previews were eagerly anticipated social occasions. Wine and finger food was supplied by the exhibitors and a gala atmosphere prevailed. The large numbers of people who attended appreciated the opportunity to view up to six exhibitions in one visit and exhibitors benefited by having their work exposed to a wide audience. Many artists preferred to mount their own exhibitions, but our staff were always available to help if requested. The rapid turnaround of events placed considerable strain on the small staff who worked hard to ensure that all Exhibited were displayed professionally and that the gallery was immaculate at the opening time of new shows.

Gallery staff

The gallery employed a number of part-time or temporary assistants, often fine arts students, who were taken on to help with specific work as the occasion arose. Due to unemployment in the late 1970s, the Government introduced a new scheme called PEP (Project Employment Programme). Job seekers were referred by the Department of Social Welfare and came with a wage subsidy for six months. We employed several men and women under this arrangement and they often continued in employment after the initial six months.

My permanent staff employed during my term consisted of:

1. A receptionist/typist.

2. Art consultant, Rona Rose. In addition to clerical duties, such as calculating and payment of wages, Rona was concerned with dealing with purchasers of artworks either from exhibitions or from stock.

3. Exhibitions officer, Grant Banbury. Grant performed the important role of presenting exhibitions to the public. In consultation with the director and exhibitors, he designed and mounted exhibitions, hanging paintings, prints and other graphic work and setting out displays of craft such as pottery. He was employed from 1976 to 1992. Evan Webb joined the staff later as assistant exhibition officer.

My staff were professional, extremely pleasant to work with and had a good rapport with artists and the public. We could not pay high wages, but it was a congenial place to work with flexible hours, and we all were devoted to the Gallery and to art.

Gallery activities

In addition to presenting exhibitions, the gallery held art classes for children. These were organised by Nan Crawley and others. The bi-monthly *CSA News*, containing reviews of the exhibitions and information about forthcoming shows, was distributed to all members. The gallery was also available for the presentation of musical performances and recitals. The Society's permanent collection became the basis of the hire collection, which was available for display in commercial premises. An annual travel award sponsored by Guthrey Travel Ltd and administered by the CSA was set up to allow artists to study in Australia. As part of its remit for promoting the arts, the gallery sponsored space for first exhibitions of University of Canterbury School of Fine Arts and Christchurch Polytechnic students.

Some groups, including Canterbury Potters Association, Canterbury Guild of Woodworkers', Bishopdale Potters, and the Patchwork and Quilters Guild, elected to rent gallery space and organise their own shows. Of course, sales made by these groups were not included in the gallery's income.

Art in hospitals

During my time as director of the CSA Gallery, I was a member of an arts advisory committee of the Canterbury Hospital Board chaired by Dr Don Beaven.[12] This was set up to advise on suitable artworks for display throughout hospitals.

Exhibitions [13]

The following two exhibitions, which had been arranged before my appointment, became my responsibility. These were exhibitions of sculpture by John Panting and ceramics by Alan Caiger-Smith.

Palmerston North-born sculptor John Panting had studied at UC School of Fine Arts before moving to London. Following his tragic early death, this posthumous exhibition was curated with the help of the staff at the School of Fine Arts. The exhibition by English ceramicist Alan Caiger-Smith had been arranged by my predecessor, Annella MacDougall. An undertaking to purchase all unsold work was not required, as all works in the exhibition were sold during the time of the show. When I took over a few exhibitions had been booked, but the calendar was virtually empty. The first exhibition for which I was totally responsible was the fine crafts show referred to earlier. It occupied the whole gallery, with large woven works in the Mair Gallery, craft in the North Gallery, decorative arts in the Mezzanine, and jewellery and ivory in the Print Room. It was reported in the CSA News:

'This will be the Society's foremost exhibition of the year and will follow the format of its most successful Arts Festival exhibitions. The whole of the main gallery will be devoted to large wall hangings by North Island weavers. The other galleries will exhibit many different types of craft including pottery, prints, and the work of silversmiths, but with only two or three leading artists in each field.' 14 Sales of over $6000 were made and gallery visitors were made aware of the quality of work being made by local craftspeople.

At the 1977 AGM President, Miles Warren reported: 'A craft exhibition on this scale with such a range of crafts and invited experts in each field was a first for the Society. It was difficult to forsee [sic] the quality of the exhibition and the public reaction to it. It was an enormous success, by far the best, most comprehensive fine crafts seen in the gallery and largely done by our new director, her idea, her drive, her organisation. This exhibition set the standard for the gallery management for the rest of the year – nothing less than first class professionalism.'

The support for this exhibition indicated a new direction. In the following years, the gallery held many exhibitions of a variety of crafts (see Appendix C).

However, over 75% of exhibitions continued to feature the traditional arts: painting, prints, and sculpture.

---

[12] Sir Donald Beaven (1924-2009) was Foundation Professor of Christchurch School of Medicine and a prominent medical researcher, particularly of diabetes.

[13] For a more complete list of exhibitions, see Appendices A and C.

[14] *CSA News*, No. 68, July/August 1976, unpaginated.

Post-object and performance art

A trend that emerged during the late 1970s and 1980s was the interest in 'performance art'. The CSA became a leader in this field. In 1977, I received a request from the Christchurch Women's Artists Group.15 From May 30 to June 3 the gallery was open to women only for viewing a construction called Women's Art Environment arranged by the Christchurch Women's Artists Group to coincide with the 1977 Women's Convention. Participants were invited to 'feminise' the gallery with music, poetry, painting, prints, and sculpture by both professional and amateur artists. While I was pleased to support the Women's Art Environment, I would not have described myself as a feminist. I agree with the thoughts of Ria Bancroft as expressed in her letter.[16]

Following this exhibition, the CSA gallery became an important venue for installation art. Also, the University of Canterbury School of Fine Arts graduates were encouraged to make use of the large space of the Mair Gallery. At the opening of the 1977 Autumn Exhibition CSA's vice-president, Derek Hargreaves reminded members of the Society's role in promoting post-object art. [17] Several examples of performance art were staged in the following months. In July two lecturers at Canterbury University co-operated to present an installation called The Plant Within/Within the Animals Within. This was described as a combination of sound and theatre.[18] An installation entitled Rape Trial Piece appeared later in 1977. This work involved a slashed mattress, the outline of a woman's body, squashed egg, jelly and spaghetti.

One of the most controversial exhibitions held during my time was the performance by one of the artists as part of the 1978 Christchurch Arts Festival Exhibition, Platforms. Fifteen artists were provided with a 15 square metre platform – square, rectangular or cruciform – on which to display their work. One artist entered the gallery naked except for a gas mask. He lay on a cross while an assistant covered his torso with latex to form a skin, which was later removed. Images of this performance were displayed on the cross. Two gallery visitors complained to the police who ordered that the photographs be removed. The threat of prosecution of the Society was subsequently dismissed when the president and council affirmed the right of an artist to exhibit his work in any form, he or she considered appropriate.

In 1981, the main gallery showed an installation called 'Skulls.' This combined sound (from a punk band), theatre, cinematic images and projection of news items.

The combination of loud sound with flashes of strobe lights was described by one reviewer as "mind-blowing."

---

[15] '(To) facilitate women's sharing in a non-rivalistic [sic] manner … not as an exhibition in the usually accepted sense, where there is differentiation between artist/spectator performer/audience, but as an encompassment (sic) of our lot as women … We wish to convey an essentially female atmosphere. I.e. we are working on how to transform a masculine piece of architecture into female terms.'

[16] Ria Bancroft: 'Like you – I also do not – and never have – felt male dominated – but – even if I had – I would not give them the satisfaction of letting them know! – Besides our strength lies in remaining women – female. However, Nola, with you, I wish them luck and some good will come out of it all.'

[17] *'We are always on the lookout for new ideas, new exhibitions … Your council has investigated the possibility of commissioning exhibitions of an avant-garde or experimental nature.'*

[18] This show received a favourable review from art critic Michael Thomas, **The Press**, Christchurch.

Kinetic sculpture was also shown in 1982 as part of the University of Canterbury School of Fine Arts centenary exhibition and again as part of the 1984 Christchurch Arts Festival, but interest in performance art later waned.

Collaborative exhibitions

In 1978, we displayed submissions for the South Island Schools Art Competition sponsored by the *Christchurch Star* newspaper. In 1980 we showed entries in the Benson & Hedges Art Award, with Australian Eric Westbrook as the selector, and in 1981 we had the first Farmers Weaving Award. Also, the gallery took part in ANZART, which was described as the biggest international art event held in New Zealand. Various sites were used for this, including the Arts Centre, the Robert McDougall Art Gallery and the CSA with paintings by Australian and New Zealand artists as well as photographs, kinetic sculpture and a performance piece.

In 1982 the CSA sponsored the National Cartoon Show, and in 1984, Sixty contemporary artists competed for the Governor General's Award. In 1985 there was the Centennial Military History Display as well as a selection of drawings submitted to the Institute of Architects national awards. And in 1986 the annual exhibition of the New Zealand Society of Potters was held at the CSA Gallery.

It should be noted that most of these exhibitions, although of interest to a wide range of viewers, produced little or no revenue. The CSA believed that support for the arts was one of its remits and continued to maintain this attitude in spite of criticism by some sections of the art world. It was only possible to show such exhibitions because of our facilities and because we had sufficient income from other activities.

But is it art? [19]

Some 'art critics' writing in local and national publications were scathing about craft shows. Their main criticism was that this was the work of 'amateurs'. If they had bothered to inquire, they would have found that the craftspeople whose work was displayed were probably just as professional as they were and sometimes more so. The question of whether or not craft should be exhibited in an art gallery is a vexed one. There is adequate precedent for the inclusion of craft. Many of the world's leading galleries include a craft section. This is especially apparent in Japan and China where crafts, such as pottery, lacquer work, carving and fabric art, are regarded as the pinnacle in preference to graphic art. Many directors and curators of art galleries in both Australia and New Zealand recognise the quality of fine craft. As an example, the CSA regularly showed work by potters from Australia, England, America, and Japan. All these were professional potters as was Len Castle, of New Zealand. Other exhibitions included Australian embroiderer Heather Dorrough, and New Zealand tapestry weaver Margery Blackman. In 1983, a survey exhibition of ceramics from the Pacific entitled The Bowl – Asian Zone toured by the New Zealand Crafts Council's Don Salt and Tanya Ashken. It would be specious to dismiss these people as amateurs.

Perhaps the last word on this subject should be entrusted to Peter Cape who, in pointing out that the notion that art is confined to graphic art is outdated, states: '... the works that these artists (craftspeople) conceive, create or programme are the strongest evidence that the traditional boundaries no longer exist. It is ultimately the works which must speak for themselves.' [20]

---

[19] Brett Riley, *The Listener*, February, 1984.
[20] Peter Cape, ***Please Touch: A survey of the three-dimensional arts in New Zealand***, William Collins, 1980.

Travel

On a private visit to Japan in 1982, I had the opportunity to visit the National Craft Gallery in Tokyo. This contains some of the finest examples of Japanese craftwork in the world.

A cash grant from the Society enabled me to employ an interpreter when I was escorted by the Japanese director.

Another institution I visited was the Ohara Art Museum in Kurashiki which houses ceramics by some of Japan's most famous potters, including Shōji Hamada and Kanjiro Kawai together with pottery by Bernard Leach, who spent eight years in Japan. The Ohara Museum also houses the largest collection of French Impressionist art outside France. In 1985 we travelled to Mashiko in Japan to view the workshop of Shōji Hamada and his son Atsuya.

Over the years I was able to visit art galleries in several countries.

In the US: New York, Washington DC, San Francisco, Los Angeles and Honolulu.

In Europe: London, Rome, Venice, Florence, Frankfurt, Paris, Amsterdam, Copenhagen and Oslo. In Asia: in addition to those in Japan, I visited galleries in Singapore and Bangkok.

While I was in England in 1985, I was able to view the ruins of Coventry Cathedral and the workshops of David Leach and Barbara Hepworth. I believe that all of these experiences enhanced my knowledge of art.

Retirement

My notification to retire was published in the CSA News in late 1986.[21]

Dear members and friends,

At some time, one makes a decision that gathers momentum to become a reality.

Last June I gave notice that I had decided to retire in December this year. At which time I shall have completed 10 years at the gallery. Ten very full and pleasant years, in which I have been privileged to have had the generous support of the staff, the council and the members.

The staff particularly have shown tremendous commitment to the gallery and great loyalty to the Society, and I pay tribute to them most sincerely. I feel that change is necessary to allow for fresh ideas and energy to take most institutions a further step in their growth. The gallery is running very smoothly, all the systems are operating well, there is a very firm financial base for the Society and very loyal membership.

I hope the gallery has increased its goodwill and has the image of having a lively exhibition programme catering for a wide range of tastes and interests. Every exhibition period seems to cater to a different group of people so that overall, there is an enormous awareness. To build upon fostering this awareness and involvement will need constant effort in the coming years. I hope the membership will continue their very real support of the visual arts by introducing new people to the gallery and encouraging them to join and participate.

The economic climate has been increasingly difficult. More than two-thirds of our financial support relies on gallery rental and commissions on sales. That we have done so well over past years has been partly due to the increased awareness generated in the arts, the increase in the value of works of art, the support of our patrons and the hard work of the artists whose contribution we most highly value.

The gallery substantially supports the rentals for solo shows and offers artists the benefits of superb exhibition spaces, good exposure and moderate commission. The gallery is unique in New Zealand in its exhibition programme. It has been my aim to have the CSA Gallery seen as a highly professional exhibition gallery and to promote the goodwill of the Society. I am grateful for the support you have all shown through your interest and for the favourable comments on the activities of the last 10 years.

My final tribute is to the artists whose talents and hard work it has been my greatest joy to perceive, foster and support and to my staff whose loyalty I have so much appreciated. Your new director will need energy, commitment, integrity, tact, loyalty, humour, versatility, vision, focus, and patience, but most importantly, will need your support. My thanks and kindest wishes to you all.

Nola Barron

---

[21] ***CSA News****,* the journal of the Canterbury Society of Arts, No. 131, November/December 1986, unpaginated.

After retiring I received several messages of appreciation, including the following letter from artist Sam Mahon. His letter was published in ***CSA News***, No. 132, December/January/February 1987.

Dear Nola,

They say that the only time a captain leaves his ship while on the high seas and under full sail is when he's forced into a longboat by mutineers or is plucked off the poop deck by an albatross. I can't imagine Rona Rose or Grant Banbury as conspirators to mutiny, so it must have been the albatross.

I remember the first time I met you. You were hanging a couple of McCahons in the Mair Gallery on nails which you had hammered into the concrete with your bare fists while balancing the entire Halswell Pottery Group's exhibition on your head and puffing thoughtfully on one of Olivia Spencer Bower's cigars. My eyes bulged like those of a beached groper and I attempted to conceal my awe by way of a glib remark. 'My goodness, Mrs Barron, that must be difficult'. You replied, 'Not really. The trick, of course, is not to inhale.' Your hair was a rich auburn in those days and every strand of it in place like a Van Eyck painting. But last week, when I called in to pay the GST on my subscription, I caught sight of you in the distance, drifting along like a small cumulonimbus about to precipitate and your hair, now grey, was like the rigging of a stricken ship.

Ah, the cost of your directorship. Ten years of buffering the shunted carriages of egoism in the railway sidings of Art. So perhaps you are right. Perhaps it is time to set a new course and fade from the scene like a watercolour painting in a sunporch. After all, there is a wider community that could be served by your unique qualifications … public-relations officer to Reagan, for instance. And your business acumen; who could match that? You have found a home for every little sketch or urchinous maquette that came through your door, no matter how unworthy, and put bread in the mouths and hope in the hearts of neophyte artists and dragged them from the abyss of despair and Teachers' Training College. And for myself? Why, the walls of every institute for the near-sighted or blind throughout the country groan with my works. But now the agonised features of Greer Twiss's bronze athlete, which has discreetly witnessed the comings and goings through your office of so many diverse personalities, has crossed the finishing line at last. I'm off to hunt albatrosses.

Best wishes,

Sam

Some final observations

In retrospect, I believe that when the gallery was built, insufficient consideration was given to its administration. Such a large and complex business as the CSA Gallery would probably have justified the employment of several technicians and at least two professional administrators – an artistic director and a business and financial manager – all adequately remunerated. I was required to fulfil both managerial roles. That I was able to achieve this was partly due to my standing as a practising artist and, as such, I was trusted by the art community. Secondly, my commercial background helped me to deal with the complexities of business and financial management. However, for any business to be successful, the cost of operation must be covered by income. Perusal of the financial records of the Society and gallery reveal a precarious position.

The operating costs were extensive and at times income was barely sufficient. Some of the cost was reduced by utilising unpaid volunteers (Society members) to undertake some tasks, such as preparation and distribution of the bimonthly newsletter. Staff numbers were minimal and salaries modest. My own circumstances were such that I was able to accept a lower than usual reward.

Some other staff members realised that the experience of working at the gallery would serve as an apprenticeship for a later career. Although the monetary reward was low, the knowledge gained would later become valuable. For example, Grant Banbury went on to establish a successful career as an art consultant and dealer gallery owner. Evan Webb, who worked as an assistant at the CSA Gallery, later became curator of the Len Lye collection at the Govett-Brewster Art Gallery in New Plymouth. All staff members were passionate about art and wished to support its promotion.

With no financial contributions from central or local Government and little assistance from commercial sources, the Society was thrown on its own resources. Members subscriptions were insufficient. The shortfall was made up of commissions on sales, hire of galleries and donations. When the new CSA Gallery was built in 1968 it occupied a unique position in the Christchurch community. It was the only place where artists and craftspeople could display and sell their work. Interest in both art and craft was high at that time. Membership of the Canterbury Society of Arts more than doubled and hundreds of people attended exhibition openings, resulting in increased sales. It was this activity which ensured that the gallery could meet its financial obligations and continue to operate. I found this appointment to be challenging and fulfilling. It represents the peak of my achievement in a long and varied career in the arts.

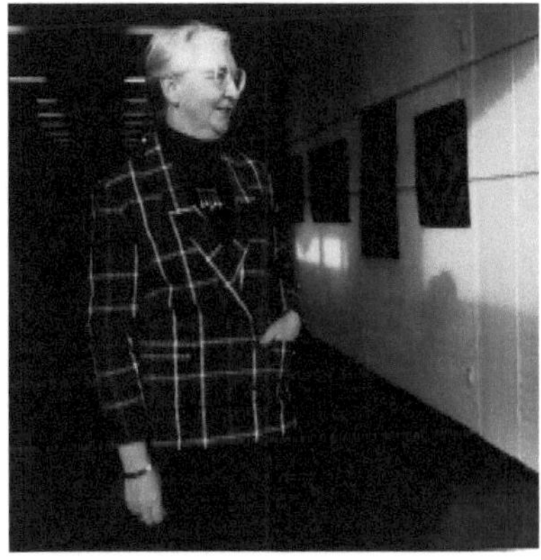

Nola Barron, Director of the CSA Art Gallery 1977 to 1986.

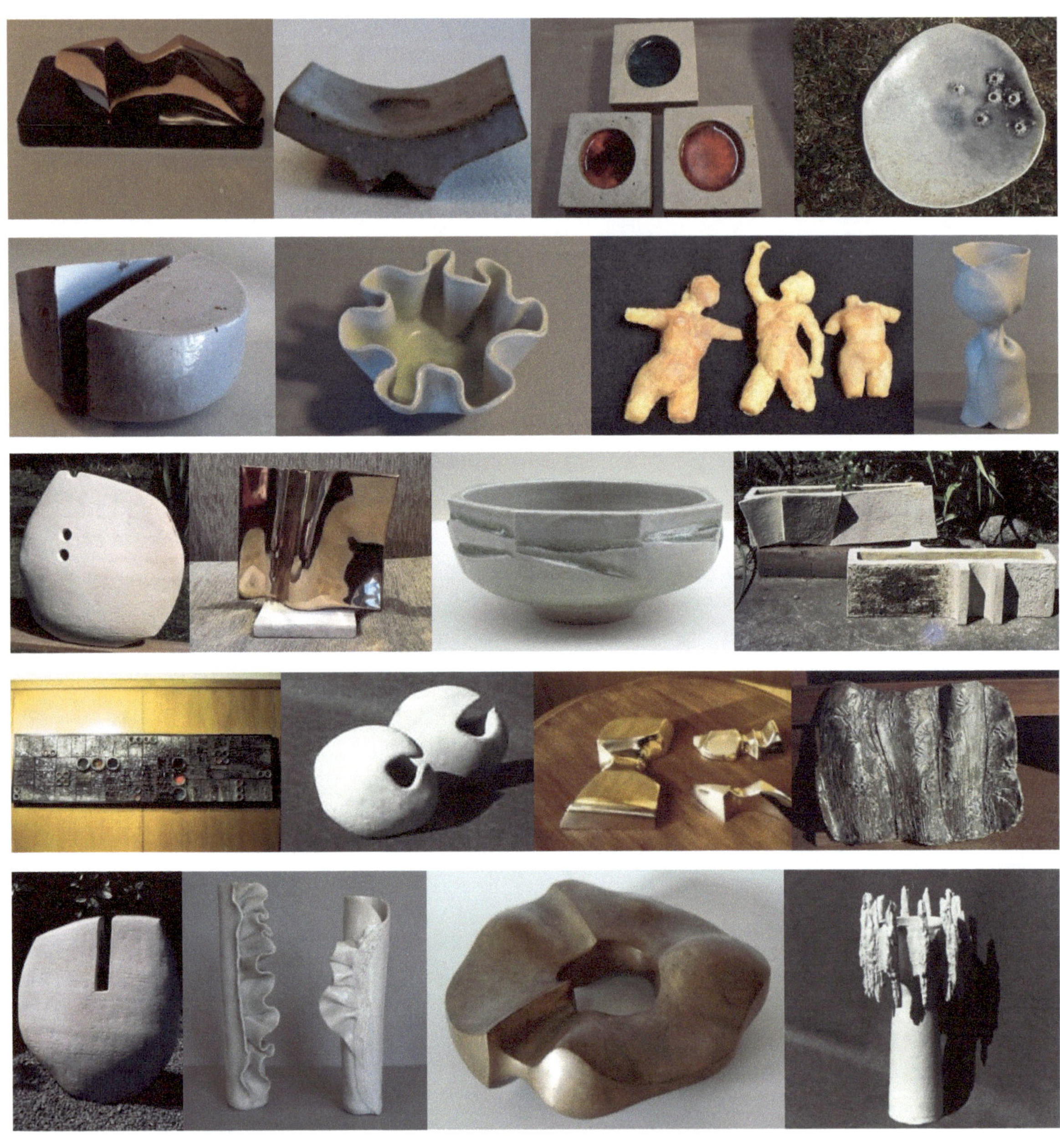

BIBLIOGRAPHIC CITATIONS

Several publications make specific mention of the work of Nola Barron. Some of these comments appear below.

1. Fired clay: the story of the Canterbury Potters Association 1870-1989 by Noeline Brokenshire. In a section labelled "Pen Sketches of some or Canterbury Personalities" the author says:

'Nola Barron, an astute observer of natural formations, has translated in both clay and bronze the landforms of the environment. The 1970s saw many "landform" pots, austere and separate, with matt white surface glaze. Clay was an excellent medium for this type of expression. In her bronze work there is a tautness, a tension which is a continuing development of the rhythm of the land as seen in her clay pieces. She was appointed director of the CSA Gallery in Gloucester Street. Under her guidance the gallery became a first-class venue for exhibiting not only fine art works but ceramics and other crafts.' unpaginated.

2. Please Touch: a survey of the three-dimensional arts in New Zealand by Peter Cape, William Collins, 1980. The author makes several mentions of Nola Barron.

On page 37, in Chapter 3, entitled "Sculpture: Beyond the Graven Images", Cape deals with the sculptural work of Nola Barron as follows:

'Nola Barron works in a variety of media and is perhaps most widely known for her ceramics. The works illustrated here demonstrate a considerable ability in abstracting from particular types of landscape their individual characteristics; in 'Landform – Marlborough series' (illustrated), for instance, there is the steep-sided enclosed inlet and rounded hill-formation which is typical of the Marlborough region ... The two-piece bronze 'Coastal' (illustrated) on the other hand, carries with it the feeling of the steep coastline of North Canterbury and Kaikoura.'

On page 99, in Chapter 5 entitled: "Pottery: The Primitive to the Present", Nola Barron's pottery is described in this extract which is accompanied by two illustrations: illustration 5/62 shows three examples of porcelain vases and 5/63 is a stoneware Landform. Cape goes on to point out that Barron is also interested in bringing her sculptural ideas into ceramics: 'Her sculpted 'Landform' [illustrated] reflects some of the landscape preoccupation we have already seen in her metal sculpture. But here Barron's work tends towards continuing experimentation. As she says of clay, 'I try to discover something, to react against dogma, to use all available methods to push both the medium and my own abilities to their limits.'

Note: For the record, Nola Barron worked in clay before turning to other materials; her ceramic sculptures pre-date her bronze works.

On the dust jacket of Please Touch Peter Cape explains the name thus: 'Please do not touch' – this notice, a rope barrier, or a glass-fronted display case all too frequently come between New Zealanders and an appreciation of their country's art.' In this study of the three-dimensional, the author is especially concerned with the tactile qualities of art: '... one should never lose sight of the fact that touch has a major part to play in all our experiences'.

3. Cone Ten Down Studio pottery in New Zealand 1945-1980, Moyra Elliott and Damian Skinner, David Bateman, 2009. References to Nola Barron appear on the following pages:

Page 69 '… the Risingholme Ceramics Group exhibited their pottery in the 1952 exhibition, [Doris] Holland's advocacy opened up the Group exhibitions for many potters, including Nola Barron [and others].'

Page 82 Photograph caption: 'Primitive firing in Canterbury 1967', photographer Nola Barron.

Page 83 Photograph caption: 'Awaiting Hamada at Christchurch Airport, 1965', images show Nola Barron and others.

Page 85 Two photographs, caption: 'Hamada's exhibition at Canterbury Museum, 1965', photographer Nola Barron.

Page 132 Photograph: 'Two Landforms, the late 1960s, stoneware, 170 x 240 mm (largest)', Artist's collection.

Page 133 Photograph: 'Ear of Wheat Vase, c.1966, stoneware, 210 x 100 mm, Canterbury Museum (C966.47).'

Pages 137-139

'While Christchurch [potters] maintained a strong base of vessels … others responded to that expression of place by making sculptural forms. Some were also exhibiting with the Sculptors and Painters Society and The Group (a painters and sculptors association) and were aware of discussions around the search for New Zealand identity in art in general. The rhythms of the land influenced Nola Barron, who made large notched forms austerely veiled with an off-white glaze. Monumental in mien, her simplified, strong pieces were an evocation of southern landforms and reflected a modernist outlook without Oriental overtones. With a background at Ilam, where she was taught sculpture by Tom Taylor and design by Don Peebles, Barron was a modernist who believed in 'the disposal of all the non-essentials'. It was Barron who, in a later exhibition of the New Zealand Society of Potters, exhibited a work that defined what a pot was, using glass bowls of water and powdered clay, pyrometric cones and dictionary definitions in the hope of engendering some discussion around the pot as opposed to the vessel, but she received no response to this conceptual approach.'

Exhibitions

A chronological list of known exhibitions which include examples of Nola Barron's pottery or bronze sculptures. The list also includes commissioned works and some notable private sales. Nola was a working member of the Canterbury Society of Arts from 1964 to 1993, exhibited with New Zealand Society of Potters for 19 years, Canterbury Potters Association for 16 years, and 'The Group' for 10 years.

Abbreviations:

CSA	Canterbury Society of Arts
CGHS	Christchurch Girls' High School
Hay's	Hay's Ltd Department Store, Christchurch (later Farmers)
NZAFA	New Zealand Academy of Fine Arts, Wellington

1963

Yvonne Rust Studio Exhibition, Canterbury Society of Arts, Durham Street Gallery, Christchurch. November 2-7.

Note: catalogue not located.

1964

First Canterbury Potters Association Exhibition, Hay's Ltd Gallery, Christchurch, September 15-25.

Exhibited ten works, listed in the catalogue as Fluted Bowl - press moulded, Incised Vase, Bottle Vase, Triangular Stoneware Vase, Stoneware Vase, Covered Jar, Small Bowl Khaki Glaze, Stoneware Dish, Vase Ash Glaze, Vase Ash and Iron Glaze.

New Zealand Society of Potters 8th National Exhibition, NZAFA Gallery, Wellington, November 26 – December 6.

Exhibited four works, listed in the catalogue as Vase - rock and ash glaze, Bottle Vase, Bottle Vase, Bottle Vase.

1965

Town & Country Art Club Annual Exhibition, CSA Durham Street Gallery, Christchurch May 15-30. One of 15 guest potters.

Note: individual entries were not listed in the catalogue.

Exhibition of New Zealand Sculpture, Pottery and Graphic Art, NZAFA Gallery, Wellington. August 28 – September 19.

Exhibited eight works, listed in the catalogue as Large Jar, Vase - limestone and rock glazes, Lidded

Pot, Small Bowl - wheat ash glaze, Pot - Tessha glaze, Flat Bottle - iron and rock glaze, Pot - rock glaze, Large Bowl - limestone glaze.

New Zealand Society of Potters' 9th National Exhibition, Auckland War Memorial Museum, November 7-20.

Exhibited four works, listed in the catalogue as Jar – stoneware, Bowl, Slab Vase, Bowl.

Mount Pleasant Pottery Show, Christchurch.

Note: catalogue not located.

1966

Canterbury Society of Arts 86th Annual Autumn Exhibition, Durham Street Gallery, Christchurch. March 12–April 3.

Exhibited four works, listed in the catalogue as Set Ceramic Wall Tiles, Slab Vase - rock glaze, Plate, Branch Vase.

Town & Country Art Exhibition, CSA Durham Street Gallery, Christchurch, April 12-24.

Exhibited four works, listed in the catalogue as Coffee Pot, Vase, Jar, Pr. Dishes.

Exhibition of New Zealand Sculpture, Pottery and Graphic Art, NZAFA Gallery, Wellington, September 3-25.

Exhibited six works, listed in the catalogue as Covered Jar - rock glaze - stoneware, Covered Jar – stoneware, Triangular Vase – stoneware, Bowl - rock glaze – stoneware. Paperweight – stoneware, Coffee pot - rock glaze.

New Zealand Society of Potters 10th National Exhibition, Canterbury Society of Arts, Durham Street Gallery, Christchurch, October 8-19.

Exhibited eight works, listed in the catalogue as Vase – stoneware, Decorative plate, 'Geode', Bowl - white glaze, Bowl, Vase, Tabletop - rock glazes, Wall Plate, Circular Wall Plaque.

Canterbury Society of Arts First Summer Exhibition, Durham Street Gallery, Christchurch, opened November 25.

Exhibited two works, listed in the catalogue as Bowl, Ceramic Wall Panel.

Mount Pleasant Pottery Show, Christchurch. Catalogue not located.

1967

Canterbury Society of Arts 87th Annual Autumn Exhibition, Durham Street Gallery, Christchurch, opened April 1.

Exhibited four works, listed in the catalogue as Leaning Vase, Bowl, Ashtray, White Vase.

Town & Country Art Club Annual Exhibition, Canterbury Society of Arts, Durham Street Gallery, Christchurch, May 20 – June 4.

Exhibited six stoneware works, listed in the catalogue as White Bowl, Vase, Brown and White Bowl, Covered Jar, Bowl, Brown and white bowl.

Canterbury Potters Association Exhibition, Hay's Ltd Gallery, Christchurch, July 21 – August 2.

Exhibited six stoneware works, listed in the catalogue as Hanging Wall Pot, Pot, Vase, "Mother & Child" pots, Bowl, Wall Panel.

Exhibition of New Zealand 'Sculpture, Pottery and Graphic Arts', NZAFA Gallery, Wellington, August 19 – September 10.

Exhibited seven works, listed in the catalogue as Vase – brown – stoneware, Vase – white – stoneware, Vase (faceted) – stoneware, Bowl - rock glaze – stoneware, Large Bowl - rock glazes – stoneware, Bowl – stoneware, Coffee Table –handmade tiles - N.Z. rock glazes - legs supplied.

New Zealand Society of Potters 11th National Exhibition, Palmerston North, September 24 – October 6.

Exhibited six stoneware entries, listed in the catalogue as People Pot I, People Pot II, People Pot III, White Crown Pot, Brown and White Bowl, Decorative Ceramic Tile - iron surround.

The Group Show, Canterbury Society of Arts, Durham Street Gallery, Christchurch, October 25 – November 12.

Listing in catalogue reads Decorative Ceramic Wall Panel, Pottery, all priced (note: individual items not listed).

Canterbury Society of Arts Second Summer Exhibition, Durham Street Gallery, Christchurch, November 25 –December 10.

Exhibited four works, listed in the catalogue as White Bowl, Cylinder Vase, Vase, Candle Holder.

1968

New Zealand Society of Potters' Travelling Exhibition, part of the Second Pan Pacific Arts Festival Exhibition presented at Canterbury Society of Arts, Durham Street Gallery, Christchurch.

March 10-30.

Exhibited three stoneware entries, listed in the catalogue as Pot No. 1, dolomite glaze; Pot No. 2; Pot No. 3.

Prints – Drawings – Pottery Exhibition, CSA Gallery, Christchurch, September 30 – October 11.
Exhibited four works, listed in the catalogue as Candle Holder, Bottle, Landscape Plates (pair), Paper Weight.

New Zealand Society of Potters 12th Exhibition, Otago Museum Foyer, Dunedin, October 13-27.
Exhibited five stoneware works, listed in the catalogue as Cylinder Vase, White Fins Vase, Candlesticks, Pot 670, Ceramic Sculpture.

The Group Show, CSA Gallery, Christchurch, October 26 – November 10.
The number of works exhibited is unknown. Catalogue entry reads "Individually listed".

Exhibition at the University of Canterbury for the ANZAAS Conference.
Note: entries unknown as no catalogue found.

Sculpture Commission for Stan J. Wilson
Three-part fibreglass sculpture installed at Stan J. Wilson's property, 25 MacMillan Avenue, Christchurch, on an exterior concrete-block wall of the house. Note: the property is now owned by J.M. & P.J. Upton.

1969

Pottery for Outdoor Living, Canterbury Potters Association, CSA Gallery, Christchurch, March 10-23.
Exhibited five works, listed in the catalogue as Plate, Plate, Garden Sculpture, Garden Sculpture, Panel of Tiles.

Exhibition of New Zealand Sculpture, Pottery and Graphic Art, NZAFA Gallery, Wellington, August 23 – September 14.
Exhibited four stoneware works, listed in the catalogue as Large Candle Holder, Vase, Paperweight, Paperweight.

The Group Show, CSA Gallery, Christchurch, October 15-29.
Exhibited nine works, listed in the catalogue as Ceramic Form I, Ceramic Form II, Ceramic Form III, Slab Trough, Stemmed Dish, Candle Holder, Candle Holder, Pot 860, Ashtray.

Canterbury Society of Arts 4th Summer Exhibition, CSA Gallery, Christchurch, October 15-30.
Exhibited three works, listed in the catalogue as Vase, Slab Pot for Fruit, Coiled Container.

New Zealand Society of Potters 13th National Exhibition, Auckland War Memorial Museum Exhibition Hall, November 16-30.

Exhibited four works, listed under "Sculpture" in the catalogue. Entries listed as Open Form, Pair candle holders and candles, Candlestick, Ceramic form "Watcher".

QE II Arts Council, Prestige exhibition, Fiji.

Note: dates unknown and catalogue not located.

Christchurch Girls' High School Commission.

Ceramic Panel

Commissioned with funds from the Estate of Maisie Hill, a former CGHS pupil who drowned in the Wahine disaster of April 10, 1968. Nola Barron was also a pupil at the school. Note: the mural is currently installed in the administrative block at CGHS.

1970

Canterbury Potters Association Exhibition, Gardenways, Riccarton, Christchurch, May 25 – June 7.

Exhibited four stoneware works, listed in the catalogue as Planter, Group of Tiles, Single Tile, Ashtray.

Sculptors' Group Exhibition '70, CSA Gallery, Christchurch, exhibition closed August 9.

Exhibited three works, listed in the catalogue as Neurons (1970), Fibreglass; Ceramic Form 1 (1969); Ceramic Form II (1970).

Auckland Studio Potters, Eighth Annual Exhibition, Auckland War Memorial Museum Exhibition Hall, September 20-29.

Exhibited two stoneware works, listed in the catalogue as Bowl, Vase.

Graphic and Craft Exhibition, CSA Gallery, Christchurch, October 8-22.

Exhibited four works, listed in the catalogue as Boll [sic] 11; Bowl 1; Vase 11, Stoneware; Vase 1, Stoneware.

The Group Show, CSA Gallery, Christchurch, November 14-29.

Entries list in the catalogue as Ceramic Form, 5 Small Pieces, 2 Small Pieces.

1970 Invited Potters, Palmerston North Art Gallery, December 6-18.

Exhibited six works, listed in the catalogue as Ceramic Form, Tall pot for Irises, Coiled Vase, Thrown Vase, Thrown vase, Stoneware Tile.

1971

New Zealand Society of Potters 14th National Exhibition, CSA Gallery, Christchurch, September 19 – October 2.

Exhibited four works, listed in the catalogue as Plate, Plate, Ceramic Form 884, Ceramic Form 899.

Note: Nola Barron was on the exhibition committee.

New Zealand Society of Sculptors and Painters, National Touring Exhibition sponsored by Queen Elizabeth II Arts Council. Southland Museum and Art Gallery, Invercargill, October 25 – November 5.

Exhibited one work, listed in the catalogue as Ceramic Form 20” x 17” x 6”.

Otago Potters Group Annual Exhibition, Otago Museum Foyer, Dunedin, November 7-21.

One of five guest potters. Exhibited eight works, listed in the catalogue as Large ceramic form, Ceramic form, Plate, Plate, Plate, Pot for dried grasses, Set of tiles, Landscape pot.

1972

Southland Art Society 8th Annual Exhibition, Southland Museum and Art Gallery, Invercargill, June 10-25.

Guest Potter. Exhibited 10 works, listed in the catalogue as Ceramic Form 1055, Transplant I 1054, Transplant II 1058, Trough I, Trough II, Landscape vase 1015, Ring Form I 1057, Small Wall Tile, Ring Form II 1056, Stoneware Tiles.

New Zealand Society of Potters 15th National Exhibition, NZAFA Gallery, Wellington, October 20 – November 5.

Exhibited two stoneware works, listed in the catalogue as Ceramic Form I Landscape Rythm [sic], Ceramic Form III Landscape Rhythm [sic]

Note Ceramic Form I Landscape Rhythm was purchased by Department of Foreign Affairs and Trade and later sold. Current whereabouts unknown.

The Group Show, CSA Gallery, Christchurch, November 18 – December 3.

Exhibited two works, listed in the catalogue as “Landscape” cast bronze, Ceramic Form, stoneware.

Exhibition and Sale of Arts and Crafts, New Zealand Law Conference, Christchurch.

Note venue and dates not listed in the catalogue.

Exhibited six works, listed in the catalogue as Split Form, stoneware; Ring Form “Environment”, stoneware; Ring Form “Landscape”, terra cotta; Vase I, stoneware; Vase II, stoneware; Small Plate, stoneware.

Set of ceramic tiles purchased by Doris Holland (Lusk)

Tiles installed in a horizontal frieze within a red-brick fireplace in Doris Holland’s then-new home at 530 Gloucester Street, Christchurch. House designed by Christchurch architect John Trengrove

(1925-2009), a friend of the artist.

Note: Doris Holland (Lusk) (1916-1990), a valued friend of Nola's, was a potter, painter and lecturer at the University of Canterbury School of Fine Arts.

1973

Canterbury Society of Arts 93rd Annual Autumn Exhibition, CSA Gallery, Christchurch, Feb 10-25.

Exhibited one work, listed in the catalogue as Sun Disc, Cast Aluminium.

Note: purchased by Christchurch artist Olivia Spencer Bower (1905-1982). Sun Disc was later auctioned, in April 1985, to raise funds for the Olivia Spencer Bower Foundation to support an annual award. Current whereabouts unknown.

Canterbury Potters Association, Arts Festival Exhibition, CSA Gallery, Christchurch, March 3-18.

Exhibited five works, listed in the catalogue as Landform I, Landform II, Landform III, Landform IV, Landform V.

Contemporary Ceramics 73, Manawatu Art Gallery, Palmerston North, June 12 – July 1.

Exhibited two works, listed in the catalogue as Landform I, Landform II.

The Group Show, CSA Gallery, Christchurch, September 15-30. Exhibited three works, listed in the catalogue as Form 9/73, bronze; Form 10/73, bronze; Landform 11/73, patinated bronze.

New Zealand Society of Potters 16th National Exhibition, Otago Museum Foyer, Dunedin, October 20 – November 4.

Exhibited three stoneware works, listed in the catalogue as Landform, Ring, Tiles – "Rain".

Set of four three-dimensional tiles purchased Mr & Mrs Ivin, Christchurch.

Installed in an exterior concrete-block wall at the Ivin home, 48 Maffeys Road, Christchurch.

Note: Betty Ivin was a potter and an active member of Canterbury Potters Association.

1974

Art N.Z. '74, Commonwealth Games Exhibition, CSA Gallery, Christchurch, January 18 – February 10.

Exhibited four stoneware works, listed in the catalogue as Wall Panel "Rain II", Ring I, Ring II, Ring III.

Hansells Sculpture Award, Wairarapa Arts Centre, Masterton, October.

Entry listed in the catalogue as Sun Disc, bronze.

The Group Show, CSA Gallery, Christchurch, September 7-22.

Exhibited two bronze works, listed in the catalogue as Marlborough Series 17/74, Marlborough Series 18/74.

New Zealand Society of Potters 17th National Exhibition, Auckland War Memorial Museum Exhibition Hall, October 27 – November 5.

Exhibited four works, listed in the catalogue as Landforms with river, porcelain; Landforms, dry river, porcelain; Landforms, porcelain; Black moon, stoneware.

Note one of the largest NZSP exhibitions ever mounted with 118 exhibitors and 426 entries.

Zonta Club of Christchurch: First Exhibition of Pottery & Painting, The Capricorn Gallery, 142 Gloucester Street, Christchurch. 22 November - 6 December.

Exhibited six works, each listed in the catalogue as Ashtray.

Canterbury Society of Arts Summer Exhibition, CSA Gallery, Christchurch, December 14 – January 8, 1975

Exhibited one work, listed in the catalogue as Cold Wind, bronze.

1975

CSA President's Exhibition, CSA Gallery, Christchurch, March 7-28.

Exhibited one work, listed in the catalogue as Landscape Marlborough Series, Bronze.

Studio 393 Pottery Exhibition, 393 Montreal Street, Christchurch, March 10-23.

Exhibited three entries, listed in the catalogue as Wind and Rain, Wall plaque, Moon Pot.

Canterbury Potters Association Exhibition, CSA Gallery, Christchurch, August 3-17.

Exhibited two works, listed in the catalogue as Wave pot, Moon pot.

New Zealand Society of Potters 18th National Exhibition, Hastings City Cultural Centre, October 25 – November 6.

Exhibited four stoneware works, listed in the catalogue as Panel, wind/grasses; 'Winter'; Moonpot; Moonpot.

Futuro Mural Commission, Christchurch.

A large fibreglass mural of repeated identical square units painted white, installed on the exterior of Futuro building in Christchurch. Note: sadly, the work was destroyed some years later.

1976

Land 1976, CSA Gallery, Christchurch, March 6-20.
Exhibited one work, listed in the catalogue as Coastal, bronze.

New Zealand Academy of Fine Arts, 'Pots 1976', NZAFA Gallery, Wellington,
August 21 – September 5.
Exhibited four works, all listed in the catalogue as Winged vase.

The Group Show, CSA Gallery, Christchurch, October 9-19.
Exhibited 17 works, listed in the catalogue as Porcelain figure, celadon glaze; Folded goblet; Folded globlet [sic], Folded goblet, Folded goblet, Bowl, Vase, Vase, Vase, Covered box, Plate, Small covered box, Small covered box, Small Covered box, Small covered box, Carved bowl, Carved bowl.

New Zealand Society of Potters 19th National Exhibition, CSA Gallery, Christchurch, October 24-31.
Exhibited five works, listed in the catalogue as Carved porcelain bowl, Carved porcelain bowl, porcelain; Carved porcelain bowl, porcelain, Finned form, porcelain; Finned form, porcelain.

Hansells Sculpture Award, Wairarapa Arts Centre, Masterton, October.
Finalist. Exhibited one work, listed in the catalogue as Coastal, bronze.

1977

Canterbury Society of Arts Craft Exhibition: Fine Crafts, Woven Hangings, Decorative & Sculptural Ceramics. CSA Gallery, Christchurch, March 5-20.
Exhibited two stoneware works, listed in the catalogue as Wind & Rain, Seawash.

Light: Exhibition of Invited Potters, Dowse Art Gallery, Lower Hutt, April 1-24.
Exhibited two works listed as: Cradle for the Moon, stoneware; Pot for catching Stars, stoneware.

New Zealand Society of Potters 20th National Exhibition, NZAFA Gallery, Wellington, October 21 – November 6.
Exhibited two entries, listed in the catalogue as 2001, Terracotta; Bridge, Porcelain.
The Fletcher Brownbuilt Pottery Award, Auckland War Memorial Museum. The exhibition closed on June 12.
Finalist. Exhibited one work, listed in the catalogue as Formal Landforms (three pieces), earthenware.

Canterbury Potters Association, CSA Gallery, Christchurch.
Exhibited three stoneware works, listed in the catalogue as Pot 1, Pot 2, Pot 3.

The Group Show, CSA Gallery, Christchurch, November 12-22.

Exhibited two works, listed in the catalogue as Eight-to-five Man, bronze; 2001 terracotta.

The Group 1927-1977, Retrospective exhibition, Robert McDougall Art Gallery, Christchurch, November 26 – December 13.

Exhibited two works, listed in the catalogue as Candle Stick 1967, Collection: Robert McDougall Art Gallery; Form 9/73, bronze 1973, Collection: Artist.

Waimate (venue and dates unknown)

Guest exhibitor.

Note: catalogue not located.

1978

Canterbury Potters Association, Christchurch Arts Festival, CSA Gallery, Christchurch, March 5-18.

Exhibited six porcelain works, listed in the catalogue as Bowl, Celadon Glaze, Porcelain; Small Carved Bowl, Carved Vase, Plate, Celadon Glaze; Vase, Vase.

Festival Crafts '78, World Crafts Council Exhibition, Robert McDougall Art Gallery, Christchurch, March 5-19.

Exhibited four works, listed in the catalogue as Small Porcelain Bowl; Thrown and cut, small bowl; Small bowl, porcelain; Small bowl, porcelain.

Note: Crafts Council of New Zealand Inc representing the World Crafts Council in collaboration with the Robert McDougall Art Gallery.

New Zealand Society of Potters 21st Annual Exhibition, Waikato Art Museum, Investment House, Hamilton, October 22 – November 19.

Exhibited one work, listed in the catalogue as Tile Panel, stoneware.

The Fletcher Brownbuilt Pottery Award, Auckland War Memorial Museum, closing June 18.

Exhibited one work, listed in the catalogue as Ceramic Form, stoneware.

Yvonne's Pupils '78 (venue and date unknown).

Exhibited one work, listed in the catalogue as Sail, bronze.

Department of Foreign Affairs and Trade, Travelling Exhibition, Brussels.

Note: no catalogue located.

1979

Canterbury Potters Association Exhibition, CSA Gallery, Christchurch, June 2-10.

Exhibited four works, listed in the catalogue as Set 9 Tiles "First Snow" stoneware; Vase; Form; Set Tiles.

New Zealand Society of Potters 22nd National Exhibition, Southland Museum and Art Gallery, Invercargill, October 21 – November 11.

Exhibited one work, listed in the catalogue as Split form, Stoneware.

Note: Selector of NZSP new members.

New Zealand Academy of Fine Arts, Crafts 1979, NZAFA Gallery, Wellington, December 1-16.

Exhibited two works, listed in the catalogue as Set of wall tiles 'First snow', stoneware; Small tile panel 'Sea/rain', stoneware.

1980

Studio 393, Festival Exhibition, Studio 393, Christchurch, March 8-23.

Note: catalogue not located.

Canterbury Potters Association exhibition, CSA Gallery, Christchurch, June 17-29.

Exhibited four stoneware works, listed in the catalogue as Sculptural Form, Sculptural Form, Cut Form, Cut Form.

1980 BNZ Art Award for Pottery Sculpture Print, NZAFA Gallery, Wellington, August 2-17.

Exhibited four stoneware works, each listed individually in the catalogue as Sculptural Form.

Canterbury Society of Arts Centennial Exhibition, CSA Gallery, Christchurch, September 6-25.

Exhibited two stoneware works, listed in the catalogue as Ceramic Form, Segments.

1980 New Zealand Academy of Fine Arts Lombard Art Award for Craft, NZAFA Gallery, Wellington, November 29 – December 14.

Exhibited five stoneware works, each listed in the catalogue as Segment.

1981

New Zealand Society of Potters 23rd National Exhibition, Manawatu Art Gallery, Palmerston North, January 17 –February 14.

Exhibited one stoneware work, listed in the catalogue as Two sisters.

1981 IBM Art Award for Contemporary Painting, Sculpture & Drawing, NZAFA Gallery, Wellington, April 11 – May 3.

Exhibited one work, listed in the catalogue as Low Flight, bronze.

The Fletcher Brownbuilt Pottery Award, Auckland War Memorial Museum, May 30 – June 14.

Exhibited one work, listed in the catalogue as Landslip (IV).

1981 BNZ Art Award for Pottery – Sculpture – Prints, NZAFA, Wellington, May 30 – June 21.

Exhibited one work, listed in the catalogue as Dark Land, earthenware.

Christchurch Girls' High School Old Girl's Association Art & Craft Exhibition, CSA Gallery, Christchurch, September 26-29.

Exhibited one work, listed in the catalogue as Landform – Marlborough Series, bronze.

Tiles & Murals, Alicat Gallery, Auckland. Guest exhibitor.

Note: catalogue not located.

1982

New Zealand Society of Sculptors and Painters: Two Decades, at the RKS Gallery, Auckland, opened August 9. Exhibited one bronze work: Marlborough 1974. Note: catalogue not located.

1983

New Zealand Society of Potters 25th Annual Exhibition, Govett-Brewster Art Gallery, New Plymouth, October 22 – November 20.

Exhibited one work, listed in the catalogue as Pot, stoneware.

1986

New Zealand Society of Potters 28th Annual Exhibition – Canterbury'86, CSA Gallery, Christchurch, May 18 – June 1.

Exhibited one work, listed in the catalogue as Cf. art, clay & water.

Note: departing from convention, the work consisted of 'glass bowls of water and powered clay, pyrometric cones and dictionary definitions'.

Ceramics 86: Contemporary Works in Clay, Govett-Brewster Art Gallery, New Plymouth, October.

Exhibited one work, listed in the catalogue as Clay Works Form/Function, assemblage, low-fired clay found object, card.

The President's Exhibition, CSA Gallery, Christchurch, September 11-28.

Exhibited one work, listed in the catalogue as 1880 – Print on mylar.

1988/89

Canterbury Potters Association 25th Anniversary Retrospective Exhibition, Robert McDougall Art Gallery, Christchurch, December 19, 1988 – January 17, 1989.

Exhibited one work, listed in the catalogue as Sculptural Form [1967], stoneware. Collection: Robert McDougall Art Gallery (now Christchurch Art Gallery Te Puna o Waiwhetū).

1990

New Zealand Society of Potters 32nd National Exhibition, incorporating United Group/Suter Art Gallery Awards, Suter Art Gallery, Nelson, May 12 – June 3.

Note: Nola Barron was one of three Selectors along with potter John Crawford and Austin Davies, Director Suter Gallery.

1993

Academy Women: A Century of Inspiration, An Exhibition Celebrating 100 years of Women's Art in New Zealand, NZAFA Gallery, Wellington, September 25 – October 25

Exhibited one work, listed in the catalogue as Honour the land, (sawdust bronze). Note: media incorrect and should read: 'sand cast bronze'.

Image & Issue, CSA President's Exhibition, CSA Gallery, Christchurch, September 8-26.

Exhibited one work, listed in the catalogue as Presidents of the C.S.A. In Over 100 Years, Print on mylar.

Note: Past presidents names listed on transparent Mylar sheet with female presidents in italics.

2009

New Zealand Society of Potters 50th National Exhibition, NZAFA Gallery, Wellington. April 18 – May 10.

Exhibited one work, listed under 'Selected Pieces by some of our Life Members' in catalogue as: Ring Landform. Note: work was made in 1972.

2016

1969 Comeback Special, Christchurch Art Gallery Te Puna o Waiwhetū, August 27 – November 6.

Candlestick c 1969, Collection Christchurch Art Gallery Te Puna o Waiwhetū.

Note: exhibition paintings, prints and two ceramic works. Wall text panels included with the installation. No catalogue produced.

Selected reviews

Nola Barron's work was often reviewed (sometimes with illustrations) by reviewers, art critics and writers in local and national newspapers, magazines and periodicals. Extracts are listed chronologically and include exhibition title, city location, reviewer and source of each review. Note: this is not a definitive list.

1967

Canterbury Society of Arts 87th Annual Autumn Exhibition, Christchurch.

The Press reviewer has this to say: 'The pottery and sculpture sections are hardly memorable, although the work of Nola Barron, in the former category, seems the most interesting. I am thinking especially of the form and colour of her piece entitled "White Vase".'

D.P. [Don Peebles], "Autumn Art Exhibition", *The Press*, April 3, 1967, page 14.

Town & Country Art Club Annual Exhibition, Christchurch.

Reviewing the exhibition, D.P. comments: 'Both Rosemary Perry and Nola Barron have produced good pottery, particularly the latter. Both demonstrate a concern for the fundamental forms of their pieces keeping decoration to a minimum.'

D.P. [Don Peebles], "Town And Country Art Club", *The Press*, May 25, 1967, page 8.

The Group Show, Christchurch.

After a full review of paintings and prints in the exhibition, the reviewer continues in bold: 'Ceramics in New Zealand have reached a very high standard and the pottery on display proves this. Special mention should be made of Nola Barron's "Decorative Wall Panel" ...'

John Oakley, "Interesting Display of Art by 39 Members of Group", *Christchurch Star*, November 8, 1967, page 14.

Canterbury Society of Arts Second Summer Exhibition, Christchurch.

Reviewer J.C. states: 'The pottery Exhibited are of a very high standard. Particularly attractive are six goblets by Irene Spiller, and the vases of Nola Barron ...'

J.C. [John Coley], "Many Paintings But Few Works of Art", *The Press*, November 30, 1967, page 16.

Canterbury Potters Association Exhibition, Christchurch

D.P. comments: '... there is increasingly a need for the work which lives in itself without justification for its usefulness. Nola Barron is one of the few who explore the potential of this broader approach ... In numbers 147 and 149 we see this capacity is well illustrated ...'

D.P. [Don Peebles], "Potters' Exhibition", *The Press*, July 31, 1967, page 14.

Again D.P. in speaking about this exhibition mentions Nola's work, stating: 'I have spoken of Nola Barron's ceramic forms in previous reviews. At the risk of sounding biased, I mention her again for I believe hers (except the wall panel) to be the best work in the pottery category."

D.P. [Don Peebles], "The Group Show, 1967", *The Press*, October 31, 1967, page 13.

1968

The Group Show, Christchurch.

After favourably mentioning the pottery of two North Island members, H.J.S. concluded: '... and Nola Barron presents works which would grace any international exhibition.'

H.J.S. [John Simpson], "A Good Group Show", *The Press*, November 1, 1968, page 19.

1969

Pottery for Outdoor Living, Christchurch.

Canterbury Potters Association mounted "Pottery for Outdoor Living" at CSA Gallery in March. Reviewing the exhibition G.T.M states: 'The most consistent work is that of Nola Barron. Her two plates are like stones covered with lichen and her panel with tiles is a good composition of angular shapes in relief.'

G.T.M. [Trevor Moffitt], "Display of Pottery", *The Press*, March 12, 1969, page 14.

And, the *Christchurch Star* reviewer commented: '... ceramics have always had a place among the fine arts and it is in this field that some of our potters are shaping very well. David Brokenshire and Nola Barron have ventured into the realms of garden sculpture which would be a pleasure to see in any garden ... "Window shopping" round the exhibition I chose the following piece for my garden: Nola Barron's abstract "Garden Sculpture" (3), (for my stone garden).'

John Oakley, "Outdoor Pottery Exhibition is A Real Delight", *Christchurch Star* ('17/3/1969' handwritten on clipping).

The Group Show, Christchurch.

Critic John Oakley noted: 'Some fine potters are represented, and Nola Barron achieves distinction with her three "Ceramic Forms" which lift the craft of pottery into the realms of pure sculpture. These are simple but subtle statements which have an entity of their own.'

John Oakley, "Art for everybody at the Group show", *Christchurch Star*, November 21, 1969, p 11.

The Group Show was reviewed by two critics: G.T.M. who commented: 'Pottery is dominated by Nola Barron's nine simply formed pieces.'

G.T.M [Trevor Moffitt], "The 1969 Group Show", *The Press*, November 22, 1969, page 18.

Christchurch potter Doris Holland (Lusk) stated: 'Nola Barron (new Group member) showed three impressive large ceramic forms in which the pot function was severely integrated with an austere sculptural shape.'

Doris Holland (Lusk), "News of People, Pots and Events: Christchurch and West Coast", *New Zealand Potter*, Autumn 1970, Volume 12/1, page 42.

Canterbury Society of Arts 4th Summer exhibition, Christchurch.

S.T.M. makes the comment: 'Nola Barron's three entries, "Vase", "Slab Pot for Fruit" and "Coiled Pot" and Jack Laird's "Bowl" are the most impressive pottery Exhibited.'

S.T.M., "Society of Arts Summer Exhibition", *The Press*, October 22, 1969, p. 22 (Note: 'S.T.M.' is likely a misprint for G.T.M. [Trevor Moffitt]).

1970

Sculptors Group Exhibition, Christchurch.

In August, the recently formed Christchurch Sculpture Group held its first exhibition in the long downstairs gallery at the CSA Gallery. John Oakley begins his review with a description of the make-up of this group: 'Using a wide range of different materials, twelve sculptors have produced works that are strange and diverse.' He comments on several of the works on display, including the following: '…"Ceramic Form II", by Nola Barron, has the appearance of carved stone rather than of fired clay. Its form is deceptively simple but visually satisfying.'

John Oakley, "Strange, Diverse Works at Local Sculptors' Show", *Christchurch Star*, August 4, 1970, page 21.

The Group Show, Christchurch.

Reviewing this show G.T.M. comments: 'Nola Barron, Helen Mason, Warren Tippitt [sic] and Juliet [Peter] live up to their established reputations in the pottery field.'

G.T.M. [Trevor Moffitt], '44 exhibiting in Group show', *The Press*, November 23, 1970, page 5.

Invited Potters, Palmerston North.

In 1970 invitations were sent to a number of New Zealand potters to include their work in an Invited Potters exhibition at the Manawatu Art Gallery in Palmerston North. Nola Barron submitted three works: a ceramic form, a tall pot for irises, and a thrown vase. A photograph of her three entries was published in the Evening Standard.

David Aitken, "Outstanding Pottery Exhibition: Vessels From The Potters' Hands", Evening Standard [Palmerston North], December 11, 1970, page 10.

1971

New Zealand Society of Potters 14th National Exhibition, Christchurch.

The annual exhibition of the NZSP was held at the CSA Gallery in September with 167 entries from 55 potters on show. Reviewer John Oakley commented: 'Among the free-form Exhibited are some which move more into the realms of sculpture, like the works of Nola Barron and David Brokenshire which exist in their own right as works of art to be visually enjoyed.'

John Oakley, "Top work in pottery exhibition", **Christchurch Star**, September 30, 1971, page 12.

Otago Potters Group Annual Exhibition, Dunedin.

Writing in the Otago Daily Times about this show displayed in the Otago Museum Foyer in November, T.E. stated: 'There are 230 Exhibited, including 33 pieces from the five guest potters. Among the guest potters, the work of Nola Barron stands out as truly professional. Her large ceramic piece takes pride of place.'

T.E. [Tom Esplin], "Otago Potters Show Their Maturity", Otago Daily Times, November 8, 1971, p 8.

1973

Canterbury Potters' Exhibition, Christchurch.

The exhibition of Canterbury Potters Association at the CSA Gallery was held in conjunction with an arts festival. G.T.M. includes the following in his review of the show: 'Nola Barron's crisply shaped white glazed "Landforms" are of an equally high accomplishment among the ceramic entries.'

G.T.M. [Trevor Moffitt], "Pottery Exhibited of high standard", **The Press**, March 6, 1973, page 17.

1975

Canterbury Potters Association Exhibition, Christchurch.

This exhibition was held at the CSA Gallery in August. Reviewer John Oakley comments: 'There are two fine sculpture pieces by Nola Barron, and rugged pots by David Brokenshire that would enhance my garden.'

John Oakley, "A universal chord", **Christchurch Star**, August 6, 1975, page 28.

1978

The Fletcher Brownbuilt Pottery Award, Auckland.

Accompanying Denys Trussell's New Zealand Listener article is a photograph of Nola Barron's Ceramic Form. In commenting on Nola's entry Trussell states: 'Its strength and rhythmic unity reminded me a little of the more solid structures of Giacometti and Brancusi.'

Denys Trussell, "Fire and form", New Zealand Listener, August 12, 1978, pages 28-29.

1986

CSA President's Exhibition, Christchurch.

Nola Barron departed from her usual medium of ceramics and submitted artwork on Mylar sheets. Reviewer Penny Orme observed: 'The "Print on Mylar" by the C.S.A.'s director, Nola Barron, certainly makes a telling statement in a simple graphic manner. She has listed all the C.S.A. Presidents since 1880. The names of the women presidents (all three) stand out boldly in different type.'

Penny Orme, "President's Exhibition", *The Press*, September 24, 1986.

Ceramics 86: Contemporary Works in Clay, New Plymouth.

This invitational exhibition was held at Govett-Brewster Art Gallery in October. Nola Barron's entry Clay Works Form/Function was an assemblage consisting of a low-fired found object (pipe) and card. Her statement in the catalogue accompanying a photograph of the work reads: 'This work for the Ceramic 86 exhibition caused me to consider how clay does work and led me to decide that the integrity of this form could be seen to overshadow the sculptural pretentions of many other works in clay, including some already in the collections of major galleries.'

Quote in "Ceramics 86: Contemporary Works in Clay", Govett-Brewster Art Gallery, n.p.

In an article on the exhibition, published early the following year in the New Zealand Listener, writer Pam Walker comments: 'Many new directions were evident in Ceramics 86 although, except for Nola Barron's stencilled sewer pipe, freedom fell short of anarchy.'

Pam Walker, "Ceramic surveys", New Zealand Listener, January 31, 1987, page 26.

BIBLIOGRAPHY

Academy Women: a century of inspiration: an exhibition celebrating 100 years of women's art in New Zealand, Wellington, New Zealand, New Zealand Academy of Fine Arts, [1993].

Doreen Blumhardt and Brian Brake*, Craft New Zealand*: The art of the craftsman, Wellington, A.H. & A.W. Reed Ltd, 1981.

Noeline Brokenshire, *Fired Clay*: The Story of the Canterbury Potters Association 1870-1989, Christchurch, 1989.

Peter Cape, *Please Touch*: A survey of the three-dimensional arts in New Zealand, Auckland, Collins, 1980.

Moyra Elliott and Damian Skinner, *Cone Ten Down*: Studio Pottery in New Zealand, 1945-1980, Auckland, David Bateman Ltd, 2009.

CSA News

New Zealand Potter

INTERVIEWS

Nola Barron interview with Damian Skinner, 2001, Collection: Museum of New Zealand Te Papa Tongarewa.

Nola Barron interview with Tim Jones and Grant Banbury, 2018, Collection Christchurch Art Gallery Te Puna o Waiwhetū.

CSA Gallery exhibitions which included pottery
1977 - 1986

The following information, sourced from the **CSA News**, contains most of the solo and group pottery shows held during that time. Large numbers attended the preview nights and good exposure was given to all exhibitions. Craft, and pottery in particular, sold very well, the appreciation of the hand-made item, its unique property and the link to the maker were valued. In the earlier years, craft shows created a great buzz of excitement and attracted very good work, possibly because of the profile given by an art gallery setting.

This brought in many people who had not ventured into the Gallery and broke some perceived barriers. It also gently introduced them to other art works. Each year the CSA Summer and Autumn members' shows could have included pottery, although this tended to reduce when opportunities to exhibit with groups occurred. The ground-floor 'Canaday Gallery' and the 'Print Room' upstairs were the spaces most often used for pottery, although the New Zealand Society of Potters exhibitions and the Alan Caiger-Smith show were two that used the two large upstairs spaces, as did the Invited Craft shows.

1977

March	**CSA Fine Crafts** (invited show included pottery)
March	**Alan Caiger-Smith**, English-potter, decorated lustre
August	**Town & Country Art Exhibition** (included pottery)
September-Oct	**Wool and Clay**
November	**The Group Show** (included pottery by Roy Cowan, Michael Trumic, Juliet Peter, Doris Holland, and Helen Mason)

1978

March	**Canterbury Potters' Association** - Christchurch Arts Festival
April	**Royce McGlashen**, Nelson
September	**Craft and Painting Sale**
September	**From Kiln and Loom**

1979

February	**George Kojis**
March	**Rangiora potters**
	Halswell Pottery Group, Christchurch
June	**Canterbury Potters' Association**
	Leo King, Auckland
	Ted Dutch, Auckland
July	**Mirek Smíšek**, Te Horo
July-August	**Thelma Payne**, Waimate
August-Sept	**Don Thornley**, Auckland

October	**From Kiln and Loom**
November	**Beyond Craft**
November-Dec	**Warren Tippett**
December	**David Turner**, Christchurch

1980

January	**Westland Artists**
February	**Robert Wagoner**
March	**'Boxes'**
	Christchurch Festival Craft
April	**Peter Hamann**, UK-born, New Zealand based
April-May	**Ann Culy**
June	**Canterbury Potters' Association**
June-July	**Beyond Craft**
July	**David Brokenshire**, Christchurch
July	**Bonar Swale and Paul Johnson**
August	**Halswell Pottery Group**, Christchurch
September-Oct	**Rosemary Perry**, Christchurch
October	**From Kiln to Loom**
November	**Don Thornley, Ian Smail**, Auckland

1981

January	**Craft Exhibition**
April	**Royce McGlashen, John and Kathleen Ing**
April-May	**Valerie Crichton**, Christchurch
May	**Beyond Craft**
June	**Canterbury Potters' Association**
June	**Bishopdale Pottery Group**, Christchurch
August-Sept	**Halswell Pottery Group**, Christchurch
August-Sept	**Auckland Potters**
August-Sept	**Studio 393**, Christchurch
September	**From Kiln and Loom**
November	**Lawrence Ewing**

1982

January-Feb	**Jewellery and Small Crafts**
March	**Canterbury Crafts**
March	**Small Format** (invitational show included pottery)
April	**Halswell Pottery Group**, Christchurch
April-May	**John Parker**, Auckland
May/Jun	**Mirek Smíšek**
	Wellington Potters
July-August	**Canterbury Potters' Association**
	Valerie Crichton, Christchurch

September-Oct **Fibre and Form**
October **Bishopdale Pottery Group**, Christchurch
October **Auckland Potters**
November **Roy Cowan and Juliet Peter**, Wellington
December **Clay for Children** (children's work, tutor Gennie de Lange)

1983

April **Halswell Pottery Group**, Christchurch
May **The Bowl - Asian Zone**
May-June **Conference Crafts**
May-June **Canterbury Potters' Association**
June-July **Beyond Craft**
August-Sep **Canterbury members of Crafts Council**
September **Robert Wagoner**
October **Bishopdale Pottery Group**, Christchurch
October-Nov **Fibre and Form**
November **Royce McGlashen**, Nelson
December **Peter Gibbs**, Nelson

1984

March **Canterbury Potters' Association**
April **Juliet Peter and Roy Cowan**, Wellington
April-May **Tile Studio**, Christchurch
May **Halswell Pottery Group**, Christchurch
June-July **Nelson Potters**
July **Rosemarie and Roger Brittain**, Auckland.
September-Oct **David Brokenshire**, Christchurch
October-Nov **Four Potters** (Valerie Crichton, Robert Wagoner, Raewyn Atkinson, Anthea Grob)
November **Bishopdale Pottery Group**, Christchurch

1985

February **Silver, Wood, Fibre and Clay**
March **Canterbury Potters' Association**
April **Halswell Pottery Group**, Christchurch
April-May **Wellington Potters**
August-Sept **Len Castle**, Auckland
September **George Kojis**
October **John Parker**, Auckland
October **Bishopdale Pottery Group**, Christchurch
October **Canterbury members of Crafts Council**
November-Dec **'Two plus Two'** (included pottery by Frederika Ernsten and Margaret Ryley)

1986

May	**Halswell Pottery Group**, Christchurch
May	**New Zealand Society Potters 28th National Exhibition** (Nola Barron one of three selectors)
August	**Cracroft Group**, Christchurch (included pottery by Nora Flewellen, Ann Davie, Joyce Hamilton)
Also shown	**German Pottery**
	Scandinavian pottery (part of NZSP)

Selected CSA exhibitions from 1977 to 1986

This section includes information about selected exhibitions held at the CSA Gallery between January 1977 and December 1986 (sourced from the *CSA News*).

Nola considers the most memorable exhibition mounted by the gallery during her tenure was the 1985 showing of 'Large Paintings' by some of New Zealand's most highly regarded artists. Her selection of the most memorable and diverse exhibitions shown by the gallery during her term are listed below.

Only the early exhibitions of each group are mentioned. Of the CSA's 90 to 100 shows mounted each year, many were regular exhibitions by solo artists or small groups, and work was almost always for sale. The gallery also held large, selected shows of CSA members three times a year. As there were six gallery areas, it was possible to tailor exhibitions by style or quality at most times. As the visitor came to one show, they were also exposed to other ranges of work. On a few occasions, the CSA co-operated with the Robert McDougall Art Gallery, Christchurch, to show exhibitions that they could not accommodate. Initially, travelling exhibitions were more frequent but became more difficult to underwrite, partly because of higher standards of curation and high freight and insurance costs. Established North Island painters exhibited regularly but later, freight and packaging charges made this more difficult. Nola travelled occasionally to the North Island to visit artists and interest them in exhibiting solo shows and was always well received. The gallery's architecture and standing attracted them, and Nola could choose artists of high repute.

1977

CSA Fine Crafts, invited, work by the best New Zealand practitioners (comprehensive and successful)

Alan Caiger-Smith, British potter, lustred and decorated pottery (the whole show sold)

John Panting, posthumous sculpture show set up by University of Canterbury School of Fine Arts. (the show occupied the whole gallery)

Art in the Mail, a travelling exhibition of small works, international

Martin Mendelsberg and Carol Miles installation, laser and audio

Michael Ebel, drawing

John Coley, painting

Artists for Amnesty

Canadian Contemporary Painters

The Group (final exhibition after 50 years)

1978

Platforms: Arts Festival Exhibition – 15 sculptors

Philip Trusttum, painting

Jacqueline Fahey, Auckland, painting

Canterbury Potters' Exhibition – Joan Campbell, Australia, guest exhibitor

Peter McIntyre, paintings (near sell-out)

Stephen Gleeson, second year UC School of Fine Arts student

Tony Kuepfer, American-born based in Inglewood, blown glass

New Zealand Society of Sculptors and Painters

Hamish Thompson, typography

Sam Mahon, paintings from France (Sam's shows almost always sold completely)

George Kojis, America-born New Zealand-based potter

1979

Raymond Ansin, West Coast, paintings

Indoor / Outdoor, 60 artists, whole gallery

Philippa Hutchison (Blair), paintings

Pauline Rhodes, installation

National Students' Arts Festival

Eight Wellington watercolour painters

Euan Sarginson, photographs, and **Elizabeth Stevens**, paintings

Leo King, ceramics, and **Donn Salt**, jade

Piera McArthur, English-born based in Hawke's Bay, paintings

Kobi Bosshard, jewellery

Tony Fomison, paintings and drawings

Shona McFarlane, paintings retrospective

Don Thornley, Auckland, ceramics

"Idea '79" – five Dutch craftswomen based in New Zealand

Yvonne and Ian Spalding, Auckland, weaving

Olivia Spencer Bower, painting

Warren Tippett, pottery

1980 CSA Centennial year

Boxes, Christchurch Arts Festival exhibition

Crafts Festival '80, included David Eeles, British potter, and Heather Dorrough, Australian embroiderer

Benson & Hedges Art Award – selector Eric Westbrook, Australia

Philip Trusttum, auction of his work

John Hutton, drawings for West Screen, Coventry Cathedral

Peter Hamann, American ceramicist

Humour and Satire, invited artists

Olivia Spencer Bower, painting

1981

Still Life '81
First **Farmers' Weaving Award**
CSA Invited Painters, non-figurative
Auckland Potters – seven invited potters
Collectors' market
Evan Webb, kinetic sculpture
Jens Hansen Group, jewellery
Ria Bancroft, sculpture
Esther Archdall, tapestry and weaving

1982

Jewellery and Small Crafts
Canterbury Crafts
Small Format Exhibition
John Hadwen, weaving, and John Parker, ceramics
Michael Smither, Taranaki, paintings
National Cartoon Show
Len Casbolt, photography
CSA Visual Autobiography, invited
Brian Brake, photographs
CSA President's Exhibition
Emily Jackson, Auckland, painting
University of Canterbury School of Fine Arts Centennial Exhibition
Jocelyn Allison, film
Fired with Enthusiasm, children's pottery group

1983

Waimairi Art Awards (organised by CSA Gallery)
Skin Sculpture, wearable art
The Bowl – Asian Zone, travelling exhibition
Iwako Sakai, Japanese/New Zealand calligrapher
Akio Nakamura, Japanese, photographs of Kurashiki (prints gifted to Christchurch)
Ian Scott, Auckland, painting
Michael Armstrong, painting
Tomoko McKnight, paintings
Mexican weavings
CSA President's Exhibition: Mixed Media on Paper

Piano recitals, Charles Martin and others

John Scott, Whanganui, paintings

1984

Winter piano recitals, Charles Lamb and others

Fibre hangings, 10 invited weavers

Evan Webb and **John Tullett**, kinetic sculpture

Leonard Lambert, Napier, drawings and paintings

Rosemarie and Roger Brittain, Auckland potters

Artists for Peace

Melvin Day, paintings

CSA Apertures, painting and sculpture

60 from 84, toured by New Zealand Academy of Fine Arts

1985

Lunchtime recitals, included Antonio Losada, Spanish guitar

CSA President's Exhibition: Dreams and Illusions, printmakers and photographers

Auction of **Olivia Spencer Bower's** art collection

Shroud of Turin

Canterbury Officers' Club – Centennial Military Display

Gary Tricker, etchings

Institute of Architecture, national awards

Ray Thorburn, paintings

Michael Ebel, paintings

1986

CSA Totems, sculpture

New Zealand Society of Potters, 28th Exhibition

Tabula Rasa, Auckland Architectural Association

John Hutton, drawings for glass screen, Coventry Cathedral

Scandinavian Pottery, part of another show

German ceramics

Martin Mendelsburgh, wool and neon installation

Colin McCahon, paintings (in association with Peter McLeavey)

Don Peebles, paintings

Vivienne and Gavin Bishop, paintings

INDEX

www.ingramcontent.com/pod-product-compliance
Lightning Source LLC
Chambersburg PA
CBHW042109030726
47599CB00002B/163